RACHE

Shadow Cultures

With love from

Rachel x.

TRANSFORMING ORGANISATIONS,
ONE STEP AT A TIME

Copyright © Rachel Bennett 2023.
All rights reserved.

This book or any portion thereof may not be reproduced or used in any manner whatsoever without the express written permission of the publisher
except for the use of brief quotations in a book review.

Strenuous attempts have been made to credit all copyrighted materials used in this book. All such materials and trademarks, which are referenced in this book, are the full property of their respective copyright owners.

Cover image by: Aaniyah Ahmed, 99D
Book design by: SWATT Books Ltd

Printed in the United Kingdom
First Printing, 2023

ISBN: 978-1-7384135-0-8 (Paperback)
ISBN: 978-1-7384135-1-5 (eBook)

HR Fusion Ltd.
Coventry

www.hr-fusion.co.uk

CONTENTS

Acknowledgements v

Foreword vii

Introduction 1

Part 1: Understanding Organisational Culture and Shaping Positive Change 7

CHAPTER 1: The Power of Culture and Understanding its Significance 9

CHAPTER 2: Factors that Shape Organisation Culture 19

CHAPTER 3: Aiming for a High-Performing Culture 39

CHAPTER 4: Illuminating the "Shadow Culture" Impacting Organisations 69

CHAPTER 5: Food for Thought – Shadow Culture Case Studies 85

CHAPTER 6: Shaping Positive Change – Conclusion 97

Part 2: How to Change Organisational Cultures 101

CHAPTER 7: Exploring the Role of Shadow Hunters 107

CHAPTER 8: Step One – Collaborative Commitment 121

CHAPTER 9: Step Two – Cultural Compass 135

CHAPTER 10: Step Three – Continuous Feedback 159

CHAPTER 11: Step Four – Creative Concepts 171

CHAPTER 12: Step Five – Coordinated Execution 181

CHAPTER 13: Step Six – Constant Assessment 197

CHAPTER 14: Recipe for Success – Conclusion 209

About the Author 219

References 221

Index 223

ACKNOWLEDGEMENTS

I extend my heartfelt gratitude to my husband, David Bennett, whose unwavering support throughout my career has been an invaluable source of strength. His belief in me has always kept me moving forward in my darkest days and he has always been there to celebrate my successes.

Furthermore, I want to acknowledge the tremendous contributions of all those involved in bringing this book to life, from its inception to publication, in addition to the many people whose experiences over the years have shaped my thinking, enabling me to create the concept in Part 1.

A special thanks goes out to the teachers who have influenced and shaped my journey, directly and indirectly contributing to the model presented in Part 2. Additionally, I extend my appreciation to the remarkable HR professionals, both past and present, with whom I have had the privilege of working. Together, we have woven the threads of the model that now finds its place within these pages.

My sincere hope for this book is that it will illuminate our workplaces, fostering an environment where we can find joy and fulfilment in the significant amount of time we spend working. Let us embrace the insights shared within and embark on a path of shared prosperity and enjoyment.

FOREWORD

I have known Rachel as a colleague and friend for over 15 years. We first met when she headed my HR team, a role in which she developed personally as an inspiring, professional and inspirational leader. Rachel's commitment to and enthusiasm for people and their development were essential ingredients as both her team and the organisation developed and changed.

In my previous roles, leading change and transformation in the public and not-for-profit sectors and then as a consultant in the private sector, helped me to understand that people, rather than systems, processes or structures, take centre stage in any change or transformation programme and ultimately drive the achievement of business outcomes. When I moved to become Executive Director of Organisational Development, I was focused on developing and leading the transformation of the organisation on behalf of the executive team, whilst ensuring they and the board owned it and lived it. The programme focussed on creating a culture which directly supported the future vision and outcomes that were wanted by the organisation over the next three years.

During this time working alongside Rachel, she provided challenges and a first-class sounding board for me as well as contributing to various people projects and initiatives. This included using a people engagement strategy and plan to develop the future culture and create a set of values and associated behaviours to drive the future culture that was underpinning the vision. So, I was delighted when Rachel decided to share her expertise in a book.

So why *should* you read this book? In my experience of reading a variety of books linked to understanding and transforming culture over the years, I have sometimes found it difficult to navigate through the various chapters because of the language and style used together with lack of clarity around the various issues, strategies, models and new ideas being put forward. Often, I have also questioned whether the authors are writing their books from a position of having felt the pressure and pain of actually delivering transformation when working as an employee within the organisation rather than as a consultant. For me, this is about authenticity which is an essential ingredient when relating the author's feelings and experience with my own.

The whole focus of this book is how to successfully transform an organisational culture. The reason for writing it is directly linked to Rachel's passion for and understanding of the importance of developing, implementing and maintaining a culture which underpins the future direction of the organisation. A passion based on her experiences from leading HR teams in a number of organisations where she was able both to develop high-performing HR teams and be a key part of the transformation of the organisation underpinned by creating the "right" culture.

When I was reviewing this book a number of key factors stood out for me. First of all, it is easy to read. By that I mean the book is well structured with language which is both straightforward and informative. It does not overcomplicate organisational culture or the transformation process and through the strengths, weaknesses, opportunities and threats (SWOT) approach used provides a very helpful guide to what works, what could work and how to make it work.

The book effectively conveys the importance of the "right" culture to an organisation and provides practical strategies to develop it. This is a testimony to the learning Rachel has gained through her various experiences in organisations.

I also liked the concept of a "shadow culture" which I found insightful. This is a relatively new concept but one which is thought-provoking and gets you thinking in a different way when assessing your culture and/or developing a new one. Developing the role of "shadow hunters" further emphasises the importance of identifying the hidden culture which may well be present in your organisation.

I have really enjoyed reading this book and relating the various strategies and approaches identified to my own experiences of developing, leading, and implementing transformation programmes focusing on organisational culture. Thank you, Rachel, for this opportunity and for asking me to review it and write the foreword.

It is now over to you to read, enjoy and learn from this excellent book.

Tony Williams
Tony Williams Associates

INTRODUCTION

As I stood in my living room, tears started pouring down my face. It was a cold and miserable day in February 2022. I knew what I had done was the right thing for me, yet why did it not feel that way? I texted my husband and told him. He simply said, "Well done."

Then the reality kicked in. What the heck did I just do?

Why did I walk away from a job I loved? Why did I quit with no job to go to? And, more importantly, what would I do now?

I was a highly competent, qualified HR professional with 20+ years of experience, and I'd been in this role as an HR director for 6½ years. But I had finally reached my limit, and it was time to move on.

This wasn't the only time when my life had changed forever. My first moment of significant change happened in 1993. After a traumatic labour, I spent the whole night in my hospital bed waiting for my beautiful new son to wake up. I later learnt that our eldest son liked his sleep. He slept a full 12 hours that night before waking. Whilst he was blissfully in his happy dreamland, I was taking in the wonder of this newborn baby, how perfect he was, his tiny fingers and toes.

I was so overwhelmed with love, then fear kicked in. What if I don't know how to look after him? What if my husband were to lose his job or he became ill? Or worse still, what if the unthinkable happens, and he leaves me or dies prematurely?

Looking back now, this might seem irrational, but at the time I felt vulnerable. You see, I had a secret. I couldn't read or write very well. I left school with few qualifications and no career plans. However, suddenly the need to be able to personally provide for our baby was strong and not being able to do so scared me. I mean really scared me. What I hadn't reckoned on was the paradigm shift that took place in that moment, and I was filled with an overwhelming desire to provide for our new baby.

I enrolled on a maths and English course at a local school in the heart of Coventry. My mother-in-law came with me as I was so scared and embarrassed by my lack of knowledge. I truly thought I was not bright enough to learn, but with a few deep breaths, I started what would become my lifelong learning journey. It was from those courses that I finally found a tiny spark of hope. Maybe, just maybe, I could educate myself.

My journey with written English has been a constant development for me, but when I look back at that 21-year-old who only had a basic educational skill set, particularly in the English language, to where I am now, sitting in the sun in Spain, on a book retreat writing this book, I am so grateful to all the amazing people that have helped me on my journey. Particularly my husband who has always been there for me, even after 30+ years of marriage.

Over the last 20+ years I have had the privilege of leading, and being a part of, lots of teams and I've observed many great and not so great change projects/programmes and initiatives resulting in many lessons learnt and the importance of celebrating successes. I've also been very aware that, for some, their job is not about progressing and having a career; they might want to provide security and safety for their family.

But my biggest and most recent lesson by far was when my career as an HR director came to an abrupt end. It is this which inspired me to be curious and dive deep into what had happened to me and the impact of organisation cultures, on individuals, teams, and organisational performance.

So why did I just walk away from my job? The truth is, at first, I did not know. I just knew that I could not continue the path of destruction I was on, and I had to get out.

Despite having coached staff members through similar experiences to what I had gone through, I had failed to see the warning signs for myself. I had stopped listening to and trusting myself and slowly but surely over time, my well-being had been affected. I had played my part, and so had the culture, and despite my strong desire to be a high-performing team member, eventually the work environment I was in was no longer conducive to me working at my best.

It is only now on reflection that I can see what was happening and what was in my control and what was not. I know now that my flight, fight, or freeze had kicked in and the stress of the never-ending speed of change and direction of travel had led to what I will refer to in this book as a shadow culture.

Not being able to get myself heard and constantly being challenged on the way I wrote things triggered something. It took setting up my own business, working with a number of clients and coaches, and writing this book to shift me from feeling like the shadow of my former self to reclaiming that strong, confident, experienced HR director that I am.

Shaping a better future

This personal experience, although debilitating at the time, has also shaped me. It has allowed me to turn adversity into valuable lessons and it has also inspired me to support other leaders who may find themselves in challenging cultures. It also provided the impetus for me to write this book.

Whilst doing my research for this book in early 2023, my company conducted a survey with 38 middle to senior-level professionals from various industries, 94.7% of whom were based in the UK.

When asked about the importance of a high-performing culture in their companies, 86.9% of respondents rated it as very important or essential, while 13.1% gave a neutral score.

The survey also inquired about participants' organisational environment, with 30 statements highlighting a favourable atmosphere, eight indicating room for improvement in the current state, and eight expressing dissatisfaction with the existing conditions. Sixteen out of 46 statements had either neutral or negative connotations.

It is important to note that the data is subjective and based solely on the opinions of those who completed the questionnaire. However, this data, coupled with my own experiences and feedback from conversations, leads me to believe that the content of this book may go some way in helping us all create workplaces where we can be our best selves and be happier at work.

This book has been written for HR professionals, leaders, and teams who are interested in understanding company cultures and how we can go about changing them. My vision is to illuminate the intricacies of company culture, exploring both positive and negative practices, and equipping you with practical tools to gradually transform your culture.

I have structured this book into two parts. In Part 1, I'll explore some of the theory behind culture with real-life examples so you can understand how this works in practice, and in Part 2, I'll delve deeper into my process so that you can make positive change in your organisation. Whether you choose to dive in from cover to cover or navigate through the chapter summaries for specific insights, I invite you to join me on this knowledge-sharing expedition.

Organisation culture is a huge topic and not one that I believe we can ever really fully understand. However, my journey has lit something in me that is fascinated by all its nuances, direct and indirect consequences, and the opportunities that it can produce.

Together, we will explore the essence of culture, its origins, and uncover the profound impact of a shadow culture, that can permeate all aspects of our organisational dynamics. Understanding and effectively managing this master culture is, I believe, a key element to unlocking a high-performing organisation. Following this, I will guide you through a comprehensive tool I have developed over the years with the help of teachers and co-workers, to help us transform our ways of working, one step at a time.

PART 1: Understanding Organisational Culture and Shaping Positive Change

Before diving into the practical process of transforming culture, it is essential to develop a solid foundation of knowledge and understanding. In the first section of this book, we will delve into the theory and research behind organisational culture, and I will provide valuable insights into the factors that shape culture and its significance in driving organisational success.

By exploring the role of values, mission statements, leadership styles, workplace structure, diversity, and external influences, you will gain a comprehensive understanding of the multifaceted nature of culture and its impact on organisations.

Additionally, I will uncover the concept of shadow cultures, a hidden realm within organisations where informal practices, implicit attitudes, and unspoken rules shape experiences and functioning.

Recognising the presence and impact of shadow cultures is crucial to transform organisational culture. By understanding the negative effects of toxic shadows and siloed cultures, you will empower yourself to address these hidden dimensions and create healthier and more inclusive work environments.

Armed with this theoretical knowledge, you will lay the groundwork for the practical process of cultural transformation. The theory provides us with a solid framework to analyse, interpret, and navigate the complexities of organisational culture and its shadow. It will equip you with the necessary tools to identify the signs of a shadow culture, align formal and informal cultures, and promote collaboration and the embodiment of desired values.

Together, we will navigate the path to creating inclusive environments and unleashing the full potential of your organisation. Let's embark on this transformative journey to shape positive change within our organisations and pave the way for a brighter future.

CHAPTER 1: The Power of Culture and Understanding its Significance

I thought it would be useful to start this chapter by clarifying what organisational culture is, the type of cultures that exist in today's working environments, where it comes from, why it's vital and most importantly, can it be changed?

There are reportedly over 176 definitions of organisation culture.[1] I am not sure how this figure was derived but I do know I hear the word culture bandied around a lot, in documents like organisation strategies where the author has commented on so many different cultures, making wild promises about how the organisation aims to be, for example a culture of well-being, high performance, or a learning culture.

The concept of organisation culture appears to have been first introduced by Schein in his 1985 book, *Organisational Culture and Leadership*[2]. A management consultant and author, he defined organisational culture as "a pattern of basic assumptions invented, discovered, or developed by a given group as it learns to cope with its problems of external adaptation and internal integration"[3].

Chris Dyer, in his book, *The Power of Company Culture*, states: "So, it is first our collective 'why' that makes a culture unique. Then come the 'what' and 'how' – what we, together, make or do and how we do it. These defining areas make up our cultural identity."[4]

Simon Sinek, in his book, *Leaders Eat Last: Why Some Teams Pull Together and Others Don't*, says, "In a culture of strong character, the people inside the company will feel protected by their leaders and that their colleagues have their backs. In a culture of weak character, the people will feel that any protection they have comes primarily from their own ability to manage the politics, promote their own successes and watch their own backs."[5]

The term organisation culture has become widely used in the business world to describe the shared values, beliefs, attitudes, behaviours, and practices that shape the collective behaviour of employees within an organisation. It sets the tone for how individuals interact with each other, how decisions are made, and how work is approached. This culture is often established by top management and trickles down to all levels of the organisation, influencing the overall employee experience. It is widely recognised as a critical factor in determining an organisation's success or failure.

You also have micro-cultures, which are smaller subcultures that may exist within different departments, teams, or even among individuals within an organisation. These micro-cultures can be shaped by the unique characteristics, backgrounds, and experiences of the employees involved, and may have their own set of values, norms, and communication styles. For example, the marketing department may have a different micro-culture compared to the finance department, and each team within these departments may also have their own distinct micro-culture.

It's important to note that cultures can also vary across different locations or regions where an organisation operates, and even among different levels of hierarchy within the same organisation. Different departments, teams, or individuals may interpret and express the organisation-wide culture in their own way, resulting in multiple versions of cultures coexisting within the same organisation. These diverse cultures can contribute to the overall organisational culture and influence how employees perceive and engage with the organisation's mission, vision, and values. Understanding and managing these various cultures can be crucial in fostering a positive and inclusive work environment where employees feel valued and motivated to bring their best selves to work.

For me, culture is an intangible feeling that you can't quite put your finger on; you just know when it's right and wrong. It's a bit like when you are buying a new house: you just know instinctively when it's the right house to be your future home versus a space that has no sense of belonging.

It is about what you SEE going on around you every day: the practices, processes, procedures, and visual symbols.

It is about how you FEEL: the behaviours, actions, equity, performance, and morals.

It is about what you BELIEVE: what your own values and gut instinct are telling you, right versus wrong, and promises kept.

And it is about what you HEAR: the water cooler conversations, gossip, and day-to-day language used by peers and leadership groups.

All these elements add to the creation of an organisation's culture.

Discovering the multitude of organisation cultures

There are several common types of organisational cultures that organisations may exhibit:

Hierarchical culture: In a hierarchical culture, the organisation's structure is formal and follows a clear chain of command. Decision-making authority is concentrated at the top, and employees typically follow a top-down approach. Communication flows vertically, and there may be limited collaboration or input from lower-level employees.

Collaborative culture: In a collaborative culture, teamwork, cooperation, and open communication are emphasised. Employees work together across different departments or levels, and decision-making is often inclusive, with input from multiple stakeholders. There may be a focus on cross-functional collaboration, idea-sharing, and a sense of collective ownership.

Innovative culture: An innovative culture encourages creativity, experimentation, and risk-taking. Employees are encouraged to think outside the box, challenge the status quo, and come up with new ideas. There may be a strong emphasis on continuous learning, experimentation, and a supportive environment that encourages innovation.

Results-driven culture: A results-driven culture emphasises performance, achievement of goals, and accountability. There may be a focus on setting clear targets, tracking progress, and rewarding high performance. Employees are expected to be results-oriented and take ownership of their work.

Adaptive culture: An adaptive culture is characterised by flexibility, agility, and the ability to respond to change. The organisation encourages a growth mindset, and employees are open to change, learning, and continuous improvement. There may be a willingness to embrace change and adapt to new circumstances or market conditions.

Ethical culture: An ethical culture emphasises ethical behaviour, integrity, and social responsibility. The organisation operates with a strong moral compass, and employees are expected to adhere to high ethical standards. There may be a focus on ethical decision-making, transparency, and accountability.

It's important to note that these types of cultures are not mutually exclusive, and organisations can exhibit characteristics of multiple types of cultures. The specific culture of an organisation is shaped by various factors, and it's essential to understand the unique cultural dynamics within an organisation to effectively diagnose and change it.

The origins of culture

So, you can see there are a multitude of cultures, but where do they come from? Well from the moment we are born, we instinctively learn the requirements of our surroundings, including the values, social norms, and behaviours deemed acceptable in society. This social process, known as socialisation, is where we develop our personalities and human potential and learn about society and culture, and how to behave in a way that is acceptable to the people around us.

The main influences on someone's socialisation are typically family, peers, schools, media, and work – activities that we invest a lot of time in throughout our lives. In other words, the person you are today has been and continues to be powerfully shaped by people and associations throughout your life.

As we go through our lives, we become part of a variety of social groups, with two dominant types: primary and secondary groups. A primary group usually consists of a small group of people with more intimate relationships, such as families and close friendships. Secondary groups are generally larger and more impersonal, whose members are bound primarily by a shared goal or activity, rather than by strong emotional ties.

An organisation is a good example of a secondary group, where employees are often loosely or formally connected to each other via their jobs, and they may not know much about each other outside of work. It's important to note that while working relationships generally start off as secondary, they can evolve into primary relationships as people get to know each other over time.

Is culture critical to your organisation's success?

I believe that yes, it is. It can reflect an organisation's soul, and demonstrate its collective identity, and how it reacts, responds, and grows; it can give people a sense of belonging, especially when everyone sees, feels, believes, and hears familiar tones and a shared common purpose. Culture can provide stability that, in turn, gives us a feeling of security and safety.

However, it can also be used as a tool by leaders or peers for command and control, which may then affect the way colleagues in the organisation perceive a situation. Their reaction to this will depend largely on what they believe in their subconscious brain the consequences to be. Even if we are told that taking risks in a no-blame culture is part of the organisation DNA and values, most of us will err on the side of caution if we have seen or heard detrimental results from colleagues who have taken risks which did not pay off, resulting in them being reprimanded.

If an organisation can create a great culture, it has a greater chance of being high performing, achieving continuous improvement, greater collaboration and teamwork, higher employee engagement, reducing attraction and retention concerns, and the list goes on.

Organisation culture is essential to the individual, the team, and the organisation and if the organisation is to not only survive but thrive it is vital the culture is nurtured.

How to alter your organisation culture

The great news is that organisation cultures can absolutely be improved, although it takes time and, sadly, there is no magic wand. It can, and often is, challenging and complex and may require sustained effort and commitment from all levels of the organisation. This is because an organisation's culture is a complex set of shared beliefs, values, practices, and behaviours that, depending on how long the organisation has been in business, could be deeply embedded in the organisation's history, identity, and way of doing things. A phrase we often hear is "it's just the way we do things around here".

The speed at which this change can happen will depend on the change needed. For example, the changing of a CEO postholder is likely to see instant and possibly significant cultural change, whereas changing a performance management process is likely to take longer to reap the benefits. It is therefore important to celebrate successes and conduct regular "lessons learnt" sessions along the way and to continually assess and adjust the culture as needed to ensure it remains aligned with the organisation's goals and values.

The key takeaways in this chapter include:

- Organisation culture is defined as shared values, beliefs, attitudes, behaviours, and practices that shape the way employees relate with each other, in their work, and with their customers.
- Culture is not about perks or the mission statement, it's about people, their behaviours, values, and beliefs that build trust, respect, and shared values over time.
- Organisation culture is important for providing a sense of belonging, stability, and security to employees. It also impacts the performance and success of the organisation.
- Culture is influenced by socialisation, the process through which individuals learn the values, norms, and behaviours accepted in society. Family, peers, schools, media, and work can shape an individual's culture, including their experiences within organisations.
- As we go through our lives, we become part of a variety of social groups, with two dominant types: primary and secondary groups.
- The types of cultures in companies may vary from a well-being culture or performance-led culture to a collaborative and high-performing culture.
- The culture of an organisation can be changed, and it's vital for an organisation's survival and growth that the culture is nurtured.

- Within organisations, there are smaller subcultures called micro-cultures. These arise within different departments, teams, or individuals and have their own values, norms, and communication styles, contributing to the overall organisational culture.

CHAPTER 2: Factors that Shape Organisation Culture

The factors that shape organisation cultures can vary depending on elements such as industry, size, geographic location, and organisational values. In the following pages, I will delve deeper into this topic, so you can gain a comprehensive understanding of the wide range of influences that contribute to the formation of organisational cultures.

By exploring these influences, you will get valuable insights into 10 of the complex dynamics at play and develop a broader perspective on the factors that shape organisational cultures.

1. Leaders

Leaders play a significant role in shaping an organisation's culture through their values, attitudes, behaviours, and decision-making. Their leadership style, whether it's autocratic, democratic, or transformational, can have a significant impact on the culture of the organisation. So let me share a brief summary of them.

Autocratic

This type of leadership style is shown where the leader has absolute control and authority over decision-making. They tend to make decisions independently based on their own ideas and beliefs, without consulting, involving, or getting feedback from team members.

They expect strict compliance without question and may be less open to feedback or suggestions. They will often have a top-down approach to communication, where they dictate tasks and responsibilities to their team without engaging in collaborative discussions.

This style of leadership can be effective in certain situations, such as during times of crisis or when quick decisions need to be made. It can also be suitable in environments where employees require clear direction and guidance. However, autocratic leadership can also be seen as overly controlling, stifling creativity and innovation, and disempowering team members by not involving them in decision-making processes. It may also lead to low employee morale and reduced job satisfaction, as employees may feel unheard or excluded from the decision-making process.

Democratic

A democratic leader, also known as a participative leader, involves team members in the decision-making process and encourages their input and feedback. They value collaboration, open communication, and inclusivity in the decision-making process.

Democratic leaders believe in shared decision-making and actively seek input from their team to gather diverse perspectives and ideas before making decisions. Team members are encouraged to express their opinions, share their ideas, and contribute to the decision-making process. They provide opportunities for team members to participate in discussions, brainstorming sessions, and problem-solving activities. Democratic leaders are willing to listen to different viewpoints, consider feedback, and make decisions based on a consensus or majority agreement.

When team members feel empowered and trusted to take ownership of their work and make meaningful contributions, they are likely to feel valued, motivated, and engaged because their opinions are heard and their ideas are considered in the decision-making process. This can lead to increased job satisfaction, creativity, and innovation within the team.

However, democratic leadership may also have challenges, such as potential delays in decision-making due to the involvement of multiple perspectives and the need to build consensus. It may require effective communication and conflict resolution skills to manage differing opinions and arrive at a decision.

Nevertheless, democratic leadership is often seen as a positive leadership style that promotes collaboration, inclusivity, and employee engagement, fostering a positive work environment where team members feel valued and involved in the decision-making process.

Transformational

Transformational leadership focuses on inspiring and motivating followers, appealing to their higher ideals, values, and aspirations. Transformational leaders are known for their ability to inspire and influence others. They tend to have the ability to articulate a compelling vision and communicate it passionately, encouraging them to strive for continuous improvement and innovation. They also excel at building relationships and creating a positive team culture, where individuals feel empowered, motivated, and encouraged to express their ideas and opinions.

In addition to visionary leadership, transformational leaders lead by example. They set a positive example and model the behaviours they expect from their team members. Often charismatic, authentic, and empathetic, they demonstrate a high level of emotional intelligence in their interactions.

While transformational leadership has many strengths, it is important to acknowledge potential drawbacks. The emphasis on visionary leadership and high expectations may create unrealistic goals and put excessive pressure on individuals. The charismatic nature of transformational leaders can sometimes overshadow the contributions of other team members, leading to a dependency on the leader and a lack of shared responsibility. Additionally, the focus on constant improvement and innovation may neglect the importance of stability and routine, which can be crucial for certain tasks and contexts.

Despite these negatives, transformational leaders are skilled at developing and empowering their team members. They invest in their growth by providing coaching, mentoring, and feedback. They encourage creativity, innovation, and independent thinking, fostering an environment where team members feel empowered to take risks and contribute their unique strengths and talents.

2. Values

Organisation values are the guiding principles and beliefs that shape the culture and behaviour of an organisation. They are the fundamental ideals that an organisation holds dear and strives to uphold in all its actions, decisions, and interactions. Organisation values serve as a compass that guides the organisation's actions, shapes its culture, and influences how employees behave and make decisions within the organisation.

Organisation values are important for organisation culture for several reasons:

Culture alignment

Organisation values help align employees' behaviours and actions with its overall mission and vision. When employees understand and embrace the organisation's values, they are more likely to align their behaviours with those values, creating a consistent culture across the organisation. This alignment creates a sense of unity, purpose, and cohesion among employees, which can enhance teamwork, collaboration, and overall performance.

Decision-making

Values can serve as a framework for decision-making. When employees are faced with choices or dilemmas, they can refer to the organisation's values to guide their decisions. Values help employees make ethical and consistent decisions that are in line with the organisation's principles and beliefs.

Employee engagement

They play a significant role in employee engagement. When employees feel that their personal values are aligned with the organisation's values, they are more likely to feel motivated, committed, and connected to their work and the organisation. Values-driven organisations tend to have higher levels of employee satisfaction, loyalty, and retention.

Organisational identity

Organisation values contribute to the organisation's identity and reputation. They shape the organisation's brand, culture, and image, and can be a powerful tool in attracting and retaining employees, customers, partners, and stakeholders who share similar values. Values-driven organisations often build a strong and loyal customer base and enjoy a positive reputation in the market.

Cultural norms

Organisation values help establish the cultural norms and behaviours that are expected and accepted within the organisation. They provide a framework for defining and reinforcing desired behaviours, and they can help establish a positive and inclusive work culture where diversity, respect, and integrity are valued.

Organisation values are critical for organisation culture as they shape an organisation's behaviour, decision-making, employee engagement, identity, and reputation. Values-driven organisations tend to foster a positive work culture that aligns with their mission and vision and contributes to their overall success and sustainability.

3. Mission

An organisation's mission is a concise statement that outlines its core purpose, reason for existence, and the value it aims to provide to its customers, employees, and stakeholders. It defines the organisation's overarching objective and serves as a guiding principle that shapes its strategic direction and decision-making.

A mission statement typically includes the following elements.

Purpose

It describes the fundamental reason for the organisation's existence and the problem it aims to solve or the need it aims to fulfil. It answers the question: "Why does the organisation exist?"

Value proposition

This outlines the value that the organisation aims to provide to its customers, stakeholders, and the broader society. It defines the unique value that the organisation brings to the market and differentiates it from its competitors. It answers the question: "What value does the organisation offer?"

Target audience

The value proposition identifies the specific customers or stakeholders that the organisation aims to serve. It provides clarity on the target market segment or audience that the organisation focuses on. It answers the question: "Who does the organisation serve?"

Aspiration

A compelling mission statement reflects the organisation's long-term vision and the desired outcome it seeks to achieve. It articulates the organisation's ambition and sets a direction for its growth and development. It answers the question: "What does the organisation aspire to be?"

It helps align the organisation's actions, strategies, and culture with its overall purpose and direction. It provides a clear sense of purpose and identity, guiding employees' behaviours, decisions, and actions. It also serves as a communication tool that conveys the organisation's values, aspirations, and value proposition to employees, customers, partners, and other stakeholders.

It can inspire and motivate employees, attract customers, and create a sense of purpose and direction for the organisation. It can also serve as a benchmark for evaluating the organisation's performance and progress towards achieving its mission.

Overall, a strong mission statement is a crucial component of an organisation's strategic framework, guiding its actions, culture, and success.

4. Structure

The structure of an organisation including its hierarchy, reporting lines, and communication channels can shape its culture. An organisation with a flat structure and open communication channels may have a more collaborative and inclusive culture, while a hierarchical organisation with limited communication may have a more formal and top-down culture. Let me go into more detail here.

Functional structure

In a functional structure, employees are grouped based on their functional areas, such as marketing, finance, operations, human resources, etc. Each department is responsible for its own tasks and reports to a higher-level manager overseeing that function. It's a traditional hierarchical structure where employees typically have clear roles and responsibilities within their functional area.

Divisional structure

In a divisional structure, the organisation is divided into self-sufficient divisions or business units, each accountable for its own operations, which can include functional areas like research and development, manufacturing, and sales. Each division functions independently, having its unique management structure, and could be structured based on product lines, geographical regions, customer segments, or other relevant criteria. This setup allows for specialised focus and adaptability within each division, promoting efficiency and responsiveness to specific market demands.

Matrix structure

A matrix structure is a hybrid organisational structure that combines elements of both functional and divisional structures. In a matrix structure, employees are organised by both function and project or product. Employees report to both a functional manager and a project or product manager, creating dual reporting lines. This structure is used to facilitate cross-functional collaboration and flexibility in managing projects or products.

Team-based structure

A team-based structure is organised around self-managed teams or cross-functional teams. Employees work collaboratively in teams and are responsible for achieving team goals. This structure promotes teamwork, innovation, and employee empowerment.

Flat structure

In a flat structure, there are minimal levels of hierarchy with fewer layers of management. Employees have more autonomy, and decision-making authority is decentralised. This structure fosters quick decision-making, open communication, and a flexible work environment.

Network structure

A network structure is a more loosely connected and flexible structure where organisations work with external partners, contractors, and freelancers to achieve their goals. It emphasises collaboration and partnerships and may involve outsourcing or subcontracting certain functions or tasks.

Self-management structure

A self-management organisational structure replaces traditional hierarchical roles and job titles with fluid roles and distributed authority. It focuses on decision-making through circles. Circles represent smaller groups or teams within the organisation that are responsible for specific tasks, projects, or areas of focus. These circles are self-organising and autonomous, meaning they have the authority to make decisions and manage their own work within the defined boundaries set by the organisation, and it encourages autonomy, transparency, and accountability.

The structure of an organisation, including its hierarchy, reporting lines, and communication channels play a significant role in shaping its culture and operations. These structures determine how employees are organised, how decisions are made, and how communication flows within the organisation. Organisations may choose a structure that aligns with their goals, culture, and industry to effectively manage their operations and achieve their objectives.

5. Diversity and inclusivity

When an organisation prioritises and fosters diversity, equity, and inclusion, it can cultivate a culture that is both inclusive and innovative. In such an environment, employees from various backgrounds feel appreciated and integrated, resulting in a more vibrant and forward-thinking work culture. Here are a few ways this can be achieved:

Set clear diversity and inclusion goals

Establish specific objectives aimed at enhancing diversity, equity, and inclusion within the organisation. These goals may include targets for increasing the representation of underrepresented groups, promoting diversity in leadership roles, and implementing inclusive policies and practices.

Employ unbiased recruitment and hiring processes

Ensure that recruitment and hiring procedures are designed to attract and select candidates from diverse backgrounds. Employ blind screening techniques, structured interviews, and diverse interview panels to minimise unconscious biases and ensure fair evaluations.

Offer diversity and inclusion training

Provide training programmes that educate employees about the significance of diversity, equity, and inclusion. These initiatives may include workshops, seminars, or online modules focusing on areas such as unconscious bias, cultural sensitivity, and inclusive communication.

Review and update policies and practices

Regularly evaluate existing policies, practices, and procedures to ensure they align with diversity, equity, and inclusion principles. Make necessary adjustments to eliminate any barriers or biases that may hinder inclusivity.

Encourage diversity in leadership

Foster diverse representation in leadership positions within the organisation. This sends a powerful message that diversity and inclusion are valued and creates role models for employees from underrepresented backgrounds.

Foster employee engagement

Encourage employees to actively participate in shaping the organisation's diversity and inclusion initiatives. Seek their input, listen to their feedback, and involve them in decision-making processes.

Celebrate diversity and promote awareness

Organise events, campaigns, or initiatives that celebrate diversity and promote awareness of different cultures, backgrounds, and perspectives. This helps create a sense of belonging and appreciation for the diverse talent within the organisation.

By implementing these strategies, organisations can proactively prioritise diversity, equity, and inclusion, leading to an inclusive and innovative work culture. This will help ensure that employees feel valued, respected, and empowered to contribute their best.

6. Work environment

The physical environment of the workplace, including the layout, design, and amenities, along with considerations for working from home, hybrid working, and off-site working, can collectively shape the culture of an organisation. Here are some examples:

Agile workspaces

Embracing an agile workspace concept that allows employees to choose where they work, whether in the office or remotely, can promote a culture of flexibility and autonomy. Providing designated spaces for individual work, collaborative activities, and team meetings within the office encourages a seamless transition between working styles and supports a culture of adaptability.

Virtual collaboration tools

Implementing digital collaboration tools and platforms that facilitate communication, document sharing, and project management promotes a culture of connectivity and collaboration, regardless of physical location. By enabling remote and hybrid teams to work together efficiently and effectively, these tools contribute to an inclusive and collaborative work culture.

Home office support

Recognising and supporting the needs of employees working from home by providing resources such as ergonomic furniture, IT support, and flexible schedules fosters a culture that values work-life balance and employee well-being. This demonstrates an organisation's commitment to supporting a diverse range of working arrangements and promotes a culture of trust and empowerment.

Off-site retreats and events

Organising off-site retreats, team-building activities, or social events outside of the traditional workplace environment encourages relationship-building and a sense of camaraderie among employees. These experiences can contribute to a culture of collaboration, creativity, and strong interpersonal connections, regardless of the physical location of work.

Virtual team engagement

Leveraging virtual platforms for team meetings, virtual coffee breaks, or online social gatherings helps maintain team cohesion and nurtures a sense of belonging, particularly for remote or hybrid teams. By providing opportunities for virtual engagement, organisations create a culture that values inclusivity, communication, and connection, regardless of physical proximity.

Supportive remote work policies

Establishing clear remote work policies and guidelines that address communication expectations, deliverables, and performance evaluation for remote or hybrid workers cultivates a culture of trust, accountability, and productivity. Ensuring that all employees, regardless of their work location, have access to equal opportunities and support promotes a culture of fairness and inclusion.

By considering the physical environment, along with the dynamics of remote, hybrid, and off-site working, organisations can shape a work culture that embraces flexibility, collaboration, and inclusivity. These strategies contribute to a culture where employees feel valued, empowered, and supported, regardless of their physical presence within the traditional office space.

7. Rituals, traditions, and ceremonies

Rituals, traditions, and ceremonies within an organisation, such as annual events, team-building exercises, or recognition programmes, can shape its culture. These rituals and traditions can help reinforce values, build camaraderie, and create a sense of belonging among employees.

Annual events

Annual events provide an opportunity for employees to come together and celebrate important milestones or achievements. These events can include anniversary celebrations, award ceremonies, or company-wide gatherings that strengthen the organisational culture and enhance employee morale.

Team-building exercises

Team-building exercises are designed to promote collaboration, trust, and teamwork among employees. These activities can range from outdoor adventures to problem-solving challenges and are aimed at fostering a sense of unity and synergy within teams.

Recognition programmes

These can be an integral part of an organisation's culture. They highlight and reward exceptional performance, dedication, and achievements of employees. Recognising individuals or teams for their contributions not only boosts morale but also reinforces the values and behaviours that are considered important within the company.

Effective communication is key to maximising the impact of rituals and traditions. By clearly communicating the purpose, significance, and expected outcomes of these practices, organisations can ensure that employees understand and appreciate their role in shaping the overall culture.

8. External factors

External factors such as industry trends, market conditions, competitive pressures, and regulatory requirements can also shape the culture of an organisation. Organisations may need to adapt their culture to align with external influences and stay competitive in their industry.

Industry trends

The culture of an organisation can be influenced by the prevailing trends in its industry. For example, if the industry is moving towards a more customer-centric approach, organisations may need to adapt their culture to prioritise customer satisfaction and engagement.

Market conditions

The market conditions, such as demand and competition, can impact an organisation's culture. In a highly competitive market, organisations may foster a culture of innovation, agility, and quick decision-making to stay ahead of competitors.

Competitive pressures

The presence of strong competitors can shape an organisation's culture. Organisations may develop a culture that emphasises continuous improvement, efficiency, and a sense of urgency to outperform their rivals.

Regulatory requirements

Compliance with regulatory standards and legal obligations can influence organisational culture. Organisations operating in heavily regulated industries, such as finance or healthcare, may have a culture that emphasises strict adherence to rules, procedures, and ethical standards.

Technological advancements

Rapid technological advancements can impact the culture of an organisation. For instance, the adoption of new technologies may require employees to embrace change, learn new skills, and foster a culture of innovation and digital transformation.

Economic factors

Economic conditions, such as recessions or economic booms, can change organisational culture. During challenging economic times, organisations may focus on cost-cutting measures and efficiency, whereas in prosperous periods, they may foster expansion, investment, and risk-taking.

Social and demographic shifts

Cultural changes in society and demographic shifts can influence organisational culture. For example, increasing diversity and inclusion in the workforce may lead organisations to promote a culture that values and respects different perspectives and backgrounds.

Globalisation

Organisations operating in global markets may need to adapt their culture to accommodate diverse cultures, languages, and business practices. A globalised culture may emphasise cross-cultural understanding, collaboration, and adaptability.

It's important to note that these external factors can interact with internal factors within an organisation, such as leadership style, values, and employee attitudes, to collectively shape the overall organisational culture.

9. Employees

All our colleagues play a crucial role in living the culture through their daily actions, behaviours, and interactions with others, and culture is impacted by the way they:

- Consistently exhibit the values, behaviours, and attitudes that are expected in the organisational culture.
- Willingly and actively contribute to the culture by participating in initiatives, providing feedback and suggestions, and taking ownership of their role in shaping the culture.
- Hold themselves and their colleagues accountable for upholding the desired culture.

- Are encouraged to embrace diversity and inclusion, respect and value individual differences, and promote a culture of inclusivity where everyone feels valued and respected.
- Are actively encouraged to provide feedback to leaders and HR regarding their perceptions of the existing culture, areas of improvement, and suggestions for strengthening the culture. Their feedback can help leaders and HR make informed decisions and take appropriate actions to shape ways of working.

10. HR (human resources)

HR strategically shapes organisation cultures by taking a proactive and intentional approach to align HR practices with the desired culture. They play a pivotal role in defining, integrating, and fostering the desired culture throughout the organisation.

It's important to recognise that the roles and responsibilities of leaders, employees, and HR in shaping and maintaining organisation culture may overlap and vary based on the organisation's unique characteristics. Customising these roles according to the organisation's specific needs and context is essential. By considering these factors, organisations can effectively diagnose and transform their organisation cultures.

The key takeaways in this chapter include:

- Leaders play a significant role in shaping organisation culture through their leadership style, values, attitudes, and decision-making.
- Organisation values are fundamental beliefs and ideals that shape the culture and behaviour of an organisation, providing a guiding compass for actions and decisions.
- An organisation's mission statement defines its core purpose and serves as a guiding principle for strategic direction and decision-making.
- The structure of an organisation, including its hierarchy and communication channels, can shape its culture and operations.
- Diversity and inclusivity within an organisation can significantly impact its culture, fostering inclusiveness and innovation.
- The physical environment of the workplace, including its layout and design, can shape the culture of an organisation.
- Rituals, traditions, and ceremonies within an organisation can reinforce values and create a sense of belonging among employees.
- The roles of leaders, employees, and HR in shaping and maintaining organisation culture may overlap and vary depending on the organisation's size, structure, and culture.

CHAPTER 3: Aiming for a High-Performing Culture

Most companies I have worked with or talked to have the ambition to be the leading organisation in their field and therefore strive to have a high-performing culture. So, what do I mean by a high-performing culture?

A high-performing culture is an organisational environment where employees are motivated, empowered, and supported to consistently perform at their best, achieve their goals, and contribute to the overall success of the organisation. It is a culture that prioritises excellence, continuous improvement, accountability, and results.

Employees are aligned with the organisation's vision, values, and strategic objectives. They are provided with the necessary resources, tools, and opportunities for growth and development.

Performance expectations are clear, and two-way feedback is discussed regularly to help employees and their managers track progress and make necessary adjustments. There is a focus on recognising and rewarding high performance, and a commitment to holding employees accountable for their performance.

This type of culture also fosters collaboration, teamwork, and innovation. Employees are encouraged to share ideas, work in partnership across teams, and contribute to problem-solving and decision-making. There is a culture of learning and continuous improvement, where employees are encouraged to develop new skills, challenge the status quo, and strive for excellence in their work.

Leaders in a high-performing culture lead by example, setting high standards, and providing support and guidance to their teams. They communicate effectively, provide regular feedback, and recognise and reward performance. They empower and trust their employees and promote a positive and inclusive work environment where diversity is valued, and employees feel engaged, motivated, and appreciated.

Overall, a high-performing culture is one that drives organisational success by creating an environment where employees are motivated, empowered, and supported to perform at their best, achieve their goals, and contribute to the overall success of the organisation.

A high-performing culture is important for several reasons:

It sets **high standards of performance and accountability**, which can lead to improved overall organisational performance. When employees are motivated, empowered, and supported to consistently perform at their best, it can result in increased productivity, efficiency, and effectiveness in achieving organisational goals and objectives.

A high-performing culture fosters **employee engagement**, as employees are motivated and challenged to perform at their best. Engaged employees are more likely to be loyal, committed, and productive, leading to increased employee retention and reduced turnover. Engaged employees are also more likely to be advocates for the organisation and its goals.

Engaged and high-performing employees are more likely to go the extra mile to exceed customer expectations, resulting in improved customer retention and loyalty.

It encourages employees to **think critically, share ideas**, and contribute to problem-solving and decision-making. This can lead to enhanced innovation and creativity, as employees are empowered to challenge the status quo, experiment with new ideas, and find innovative solutions to organisational challenges.

This culture can **improve customer satisfaction**, as employees are motivated and empowered to provide excellent service and meet customer needs. Engaged and high-performing employees are more likely to go the extra mile to exceed customer expectations, resulting in improved customer retention and loyalty.

Organisations with a strong high-performing culture are **more likely to attract and retain top talent**. High-performing employees are often attracted to organisations that prioritise performance, accountability, and excellence, and are willing to invest in their growth and development.

When employees consistently perform at their best, organisations are more likely to achieve their strategic objectives, outperform competitors, and stay ahead in a rapidly changing business environment, giving them the **all-important competitive advantage** in the marketplace.

Overall, a high-performing culture is important because it drives organisational success by creating an environment where employees are motivated, engaged, and empowered to consistently perform at their best, leading to improved performance, innovation, customer satisfaction, and talent attraction.

What type of high-performing cultures exist in today's companies?

In Chapter 1, I gave a sample of different types of company cultures in order to give you an overall understanding. Now I would like us to focus in more detail on some of the different types of high-performing cultures that exist within organisations. These cultures are shaped by different factors, including industry, organisational values, leadership styles, and employee demographics.

While each high-performing culture is unique, they share common characteristics that drive exceptional performance and success. Let's explore some of the prominent types of high-performing cultures and some well-known examples of companies that appear to exhibit these characteristics (please note that these case studies are subjective and may not form everybody's views of these companies).

Disclaimer: The following case studies are based on my interpretation of available information, and their complexity may not be fully captured. They are presented solely to illustrate how these cultures can work in practice.

Performance-driven culture

This type of high-performing culture places a strong emphasis on achieving and surpassing performance targets and goals. Organisations with a performance-driven culture foster a results-oriented environment where individuals are motivated to deliver outstanding outcomes. They set ambitious benchmarks, reward achievement, and promote a sense of accountability and healthy competition.

Case study: Google – a performance-driven culture

Google, a multinational technology company, is renowned for its performance-driven culture that has propelled it to be a global leader in the digital industry. The company's success can be attributed to its strong emphasis on achieving exceptional results and fostering a high-performing work environment.

At Google, a performance-driven culture is embedded in the company's DNA. From the recruitment process to daily operations, employees are encouraged to strive for excellence and surpass performance targets. The company sets ambitious goals and objectives, pushing individuals and teams to continuously innovate and deliver outstanding outcomes.

Accountability is a key pillar of Google's performance-driven culture. Employees are empowered to take ownership of their work and are held responsible for delivering results. Clear expectations are set, and performance goals are aligned with the company's strategic priorities. Managers provide ongoing support, guidance, and coaching to ensure employees have the necessary resources and skills to excel in their roles.

Google's performance-driven culture is supported by a comprehensive performance management system. Regular performance evaluations and feedback sessions are conducted to assess employee performance, identify areas of improvement, and recognise exceptional achievements. High performers are rewarded with bonuses, promotions, and opportunities for career advancement, creating a culture of high achievement and motivation.

In addition to individual performance, Google promotes collaborative excellence. While individuals are encouraged to strive for personal success, teamwork and cross-functional collaboration are highly valued. The company fosters a culture of knowledge sharing, where employees are encouraged to learn from each other and leverage their collective expertise to drive innovation and solve complex problems.

Google nurtures a healthy sense of competition among its employees. The company organises internal challenges, hackathons, and innovation competitions to fuel creativity and inspire breakthrough ideas. This healthy competition not only drives individual performance but also spurs collective achievements, fostering a culture of continuous improvement and innovation.

The success of Google's performance-driven culture can be seen in its market dominance, innovative products, and strong financial performance. The company's ability to attract top talent and retain high-performing employees is a testament to the effectiveness of its performance-driven culture.

Innovation and creativity culture

This type of high-performing culture values and nurtures ideas, embraces experimentation, and supports a mindset of continuous improvement. It encourages employees to think outside the box, take calculated risks, and seek innovative and creative solutions to challenges.

Case study: Pixar Animation Studios – an innovation and creativity culture

Pixar Animation Studios, known for its ground-breaking animated films, exemplifies an innovation and creativity culture that has been instrumental in its success and industry leadership. The company's commitment to fostering a creative and innovative environment has resulted in numerous award-winning films and technological advancements.

At Pixar, innovation and creativity are deeply ingrained in the company's core values and practices. The company embraces a culture that encourages employees at all levels to contribute ideas, experiment with new concepts, and push the boundaries of storytelling and animation. Pixar's leaders understand that creativity thrives in an environment where individuals feel empowered, inspired, and supported.

One of the key elements of Pixar's innovation and creativity culture is the concept of "plussing". This approach encourages employees to build upon ideas and make them even better through collaboration and constructive feedback. Teams engage in open discussions, brainstorming sessions, and peer reviews to refine concepts and enhance creative solutions. This collaborative and iterative process allows for continuous improvement and encourages a culture of collective creativity.

Pixar promotes a mindset of risk-taking and learning from failure. The company recognises that not every idea will succeed, but it values the process of experimentation and the lessons learned along the way. Employees are encouraged to take calculated risks, challenge conventional thinking, and explore unconventional approaches to problem-solving. This willingness to embrace failure as a part of the creative process has fostered an environment where innovation thrives.

To support innovation and creativity, Pixar provides its employees with the necessary resources and tools. The company invests in state-of-the-art technology, research and development, and ongoing training to nurture talent and push the boundaries of animation. Pixar also fosters a culture of continuous learning, encouraging employees to explore new skills, attend workshops, and participate in industry conferences to stay at the forefront of their respective fields.

Furthermore, Pixar promotes cross-functional collaboration and diversity of thought. Teams comprised of individuals from different backgrounds and disciplines come together to tackle creative challenges. This diversity sparks fresh perspectives and allows for the fusion of ideas from various sources, resulting in innovative and ground-breaking storytelling.

The success of Pixar's innovation and creativity culture can be witnessed in its string of critically acclaimed films and its impact on the animation industry. The company's ability to consistently deliver compelling stories, memorable characters, and technological advancements is a testament to its commitment to nurturing an environment where innovation and creativity can thrive.

Collaborative culture

Collaboration is a hallmark of high-performing cultures that thrive on teamwork and effective communication. These organisations prioritise collaboration and foster a sense of collective responsibility. They create platforms and structures that facilitate cross-functional collaboration, knowledge sharing, and the seamless flow of information. A collaborative culture encourages employees to leverage each other's strengths, work together towards common goals, and drive collective success.

Case study: Innocent Drinks – a collaborative culture

Innocent Drinks, a well-known British beverage company, has developed a collaborative culture that has played a significant role in its success and growth. The company is recognised for its innovative and healthy products, and its collaborative approach is deeply ingrained in its operations, core values, and practices. The company believes that great ideas and breakthrough innovations can emerge when people work together and share their expertise. This collaborative mindset is evident in various aspects of the company's culture.

One of the key elements of Innocent Drinks' collaborative culture is its inclusive decision-making process. The company actively seeks input and ideas from employees at all levels, irrespective of their roles or titles. Regular team meetings, brainstorming sessions, and cross-functional collaborations provide platforms for employees to share their perspectives, contribute ideas, and collectively solve challenges. This inclusive decision-making approach fosters a sense of ownership and accountability among employees, driving collaboration and innovation.

Innocent Drinks also promotes a flat organisational structure, where hierarchies are minimised, and open communication channels are established. Employees are encouraged to interact and collaborate with colleagues across different departments, enabling knowledge sharing and cross-pollination of ideas. The company's physical office space is designed to facilitate collaboration, with open work areas, communal spaces, and shared meeting rooms that encourage spontaneous interactions and idea exchanges.

To further foster collaboration, Innocent Drinks has implemented various internal communication tools and platforms. These digital tools enable employees to connect, share information, and collaborate regardless of their physical location. The company utilises online collaboration platforms, instant messaging tools, and project management software to streamline communication and enable efficient collaboration on projects and initiatives.

Innocent Drinks also invests in team-building activities and initiatives to strengthen collaboration and build strong relationships among employees. Regular team-building exercises, off-site retreats, and social events create opportunities for employees to bond, collaborate, and develop a sense of camaraderie. These activities help break down barriers and silos, promoting collaboration and teamwork across the organisation.

The success of Innocent Drinks' collaborative culture can be seen in its innovative product offerings and market presence. The company continuously introduces new and exciting beverage options, driven by the collaborative efforts of its employees. By fostering a culture where collaboration is valued and encouraged, Innocent Drinks has been able to tap into the collective creativity and expertise of its workforce, leading to the development of unique and successful product lines.

Customer-centric culture

Organisations with a customer-centric culture place a strong emphasis on understanding and meeting customer needs. They prioritise delivering exceptional customer experiences and align their strategies and processes accordingly. These cultures encourage a customer-focused mindset among employees, empowering them to go above and beyond to exceed customer expectations and build long-term relationships.

Case study: John Lewis – a customer-centric culture

John Lewis, a well-known British retail company, has established a strong customer-centric culture that has been instrumental in its success and reputation. The company's commitment to creating exceptional customer experiences is at the core of their business strategy and deeply ingrained in its values and operations. The company recognises that satisfied and loyal customers are the key to long-term success. To cultivate a customer-centric culture, John Lewis has implemented several practices and initiatives.

The company focuses on understanding customer needs by investing in extensive market research and customer feedback mechanisms to gain insights into customer preferences, expectations, and pain points. This information is used to shape product offerings, tailor services, and improve the overall customer experience.

John Lewis places a strong emphasis on delivering personalised and tailored experiences to its customers. The company's employees are trained to actively listen to customers, understand their unique requirements, and provide relevant and personalised recommendations. The company also values the feedback and input of its customers, actively seeking their opinions and suggestions to continually enhance its offerings.

To ensure a seamless and consistent customer experience, John Lewis has implemented cross-functional collaboration and communication. Different departments within the company work together to ensure a unified approach to customer service. This collaborative effort enables the sharing of customer insights, alignment of strategies, and coordinated actions to deliver exceptional service at every touchpoint.

Employee empowerment is another crucial aspect of John Lewis' customer-centric culture. The company recognises that engaged and motivated employees are more likely to provide exceptional customer service. John Lewis invests in training and development programmes to equip employees with the necessary skills and knowledge to deliver outstanding customer experiences. Employees are empowered to make decisions that prioritise customer satisfaction, fostering a sense of ownership and accountability.

In addition, John Lewis embraces a long-term perspective in its customer relationships. The company focuses on building connections with customers, aiming for repeat business and customer loyalty. This customer-centric approach is evident in the company's generous return policies, commitment to resolving customer issues promptly, and personalised follow-up communications to ensure ongoing customer satisfaction.

The success of John Lewis' customer-centric culture is reflected in its strong brand reputation and customer loyalty. The company has consistently been recognised for its exceptional customer service and is known for its commitment to putting the customer at the heart of its operations. By fostering a culture that prioritises customer needs, John Lewis has been able to build customer relationships and maintain a competitive edge in the UK retail industry.

Learning and development culture

High-performing cultures that prioritise continuous learning and development recognise the importance of investing in their employees' growth. They provide opportunities for skill development, training, and career advancement. These organisations foster a culture of curiosity, encourage knowledge sharing, and embrace a growth mindset. They understand that nurturing their employees' potential leads to enhanced performance and adaptability in an ever-changing business landscape.

Case study: Unilever – a learning and development culture

Unilever, a multinational British consumer goods company, recognises that investing in employee growth and skill development is essential for maintaining a competitive edge and driving innovation.

The company offers a wide range of learning opportunities and resources to its employees, empowering them to continuously enhance their skills and knowledge. Unilever's learning programmes cover various areas, including leadership development, technical training, and functional expertise.

One of the key aspects of Unilever's learning and development culture is its focus on individual growth and career advancement. The company provides employees with clear development pathways and opportunities to expand their capabilities. Unilever offers a range of training programmes, mentoring initiatives, and job rotations to help employees acquire new skills, broaden their experiences, and progress in their careers.

Unilever also embraces a culture of curiosity and knowledge sharing. The company encourages employees to explore new ideas, challenge the status quo, and learn from one another. Unilever promotes internal collaboration and networking through platforms that facilitate knowledge exchange and best practice sharing. This collaborative environment fosters a sense of community and empowers employees to contribute their unique perspectives and expertise.

In addition to formal training programmes, Unilever emphasises informal learning and experiential opportunities. The company encourages employees to take on challenging assignments, stretch projects, and cross-functional collaborations. These experiences provide valuable learning opportunities and enable employees to develop new skills and capabilities through hands-on experiences.

Unilever's learning and development culture is supported by strong leadership commitment. The company's leaders actively promote and participate in learning initiatives, serving as role models for continuous growth and development. Unilever's leaders prioritise coaching and mentoring, providing guidance and support to help employees reach their full potential.

The impact of Unilever's learning and development culture is evident in the company's performance and innovation. By investing in employee growth and skills development, Unilever has nurtured a workforce that is adaptable, agile, and equipped to navigate the evolving business landscape. The company's commitment to learning and development has contributed to its ability to innovate and stay ahead in the highly competitive consumer goods industry.

Ethical and values-driven culture

A high-performing culture rooted in strong ethics and values is essential for sustainable success. Organisations with this type of culture prioritise integrity, transparency, and ethical decision-making. They cultivate a shared sense of purpose and a commitment to doing what is right. These organisations attract and retain employees who align with their values, creating a positive and principled work environment.

Case study: The Body Shop – an ethical and values-driven culture

The Body Shop, a well-known UK-based cosmetics and skincare company, has long been recognised for its commitment to ethical practices and values-driven culture. The company's core values of activism, environmental sustainability, and social responsibility are deeply embedded in its operations, guiding its decision-making and shaping its organisational culture.

The company is dedicated to sourcing natural ingredients responsibly, supporting fair trade, and promoting cruelty-free products. They have taken a strong stance against animal testing in the beauty industry and advocate for sustainable sourcing practices. The Body Shop's ethical commitments resonate with employees, customers, and stakeholders, creating a sense of purpose and pride in being part of a company that values integrity and social impact.

The company's values-driven culture is nurtured through various initiatives and programmes. The Body Shop encourages employee engagement and participation in ethical campaigns and charitable activities. They provide opportunities for employees to volunteer, engage in community outreach, and contribute to causes aligned with the company's values. This culture of activism fosters a strong sense of shared purpose and creates a positive impact beyond the workplace.

Transparency and open communication are also integral to The Body Shop's values-driven culture. The company actively communicates its ethical practices, initiatives, and progress to employees, customers, and stakeholders. They are transparent about their supply chain, sustainability efforts, and community partnerships. This transparency builds trust and reinforces the company's commitment to living up to its values.

The Body Shop's values-driven culture has a profound impact on its brand identity and customer loyalty. Consumers who prioritise ethical and sustainable choices are drawn to The Body Shop's products, knowing that their purchase supports a company that aligns with their values. The company's commitment to social and environmental causes resonates with customers, contributing to a strong brand reputation and customer advocacy.

It's important to note that these types of high-performing cultures are not mutually exclusive, and many organisations embody a combination of these characteristics. The specific blend of cultures depends on the organisation's vision, mission, and strategic priorities. By understanding the different types of high-performing cultures, organisations can tailor their approaches to cultivate a culture that aligns with their unique needs and aspirations.

How can you create a high-performing culture?

Creating a high-performing culture is a deliberate and intentional process that requires effort, leadership commitment, and ongoing dedication. While each organisation's journey may differ, there are some key strategies and practices that can help in creating a high-performing culture:

Start by clearly defining the core values and behavioural expectations that align with the organisation's vision and goals. These values should guide decision-making, actions, and interactions within the organisation. Communicate these values consistently and reinforce them through various channels, such as organisation-wide meetings, internal communications, and training programmes.

As I have already mentioned, leaders play a crucial role in shaping and modelling the desired culture. They must embody the values and behaviours they expect from employees. Leaders should consistently demonstrate integrity, transparency, and accountability. By leading by example, leaders inspire and motivate employees to emulate these qualities, creating a ripple effect throughout the organisation.

Establish a culture of open and transparent communication where employees feel safe to voice their ideas, concerns, and feedback. Encourage two-way communication channels, such as regular team meetings, suggestion boxes, or anonymous feedback mechanisms. Actively listen to employees and respond to their input. Effective communication builds trust, encourages collaboration, and creates a sense of belonging.

Provide employees with the necessary tools, resources, and autonomy to excel in their roles. Encourage professional development and offer opportunities for growth. Support employees in acquiring new skills, expanding their knowledge, and taking on challenging assignments. By empowering employees, organisations foster a sense of ownership, engagement, and a commitment to continuous improvement.

Create a culture of recognition and rewards to acknowledge and celebrate exceptional performance and contributions. Implement fair and consistent performance evaluation processes that align with the organisation's values and goals. Recognise employees for their achievements publicly, whether through awards, appreciation events, or public acknowledgements. Meaningful recognition reinforces positive behaviours and motivates others to strive for excellence.

Encourage teamwork by breaking down silos and promoting cross-functional working. Establish clear goals and objectives that require collaboration between teams or departments. Foster a sense of collective responsibility and encourage knowledge sharing and cooperation. Create opportunities for employees to work on cross-functional projects or participate in team-building activities.

Cultivate a culture of innovation by encouraging employees to challenge the status quo, share their ideas, and experiment with new approaches. Provide platforms for sharing knowledge and best practices across the organisation. Foster a learning mindset by supporting continuous learning and development opportunities. Encourage employees to stay abreast of industry trends and technologies.

Regularly assess the effectiveness of the culture and its impact on organisational performance. Seek feedback from employees through surveys, focus groups, or one-on-one discussions. Monitor key performance indicators and assess whether the culture supports desired outcomes. Be open to feedback and be willing to make necessary adjustments and improvements to ensure the culture remains aligned with organisational goals.

Creating a high-performing culture is an ongoing journey that requires consistent effort and attention. It involves aligning values, behaviours, and practices to support the organisation's strategic objectives. By investing in creating a positive and engaging culture, organisations can foster employee satisfaction, attract top talent, and drive sustained performance and success.

Overall impact of a high-performing culture

Strengths

A high-performing culture brings several strengths and advantages to organisations. Here are some key strengths associated with a high-performing culture:

» High-performing cultures prioritise employee engagement, ensuring that employees feel valued, supported, and connected to the organisation's mission and vision. Engaged employees are more committed to their work, exhibit higher levels of discretionary effort, and are more likely to go the extra mile to achieve organisational objectives.

» Organisations with a high-performing culture are attractive to top talent. A positive reputation for a high-performing culture can help attract high-calibre candidates who seek a challenging and rewarding work environment. Moreover, employees are more likely to stay with an organisation that values and supports their growth, leading to improved employee retention rates.
» A high-performing culture emphasises collaboration and teamwork, breaking down silos and fostering effective communication and cooperation between individuals and teams. Employees work together towards shared goals, leveraging their diverse skills and perspectives to drive innovation and achieve superior outcomes.
» High-performing cultures are closely aligned with organisational goals, values, and strategies. Employees understand how their work contributes to the overall success of the organisation, creating a sense of purpose and direction. This alignment ensures that efforts are focused on the most critical priorities and helps drive progress towards strategic objectives.
» In a high-performing culture, learning and development are prioritised. Organisations invest in training programmes, mentorship initiatives, and opportunities for skill enhancement. This commitment to continuous learning helps employees develop new competencies, adapt to evolving market demands, and stay ahead of the competition.
» Organisations with a high-performing culture often enjoy a positive reputation within their industry and among stakeholders. A strong culture can enhance the organisation's brand image, attract business partnerships, and build trust with customers and clients.

By leveraging these strengths, organisations can achieve a sustainable competitive advantage, drive innovation, and create a positive and fulfilling work environment for their employees.

Weaknesses

While high-performing cultures offer numerous strengths, it's important to acknowledge that they may also have certain weaknesses. Recognising these weaknesses can help organisations address them and further enhance their culture. Some potential weaknesses associated with high-performing cultures are:

- In a high-performing culture, there can be a strong drive to excel and achieve ambitious goals. This can sometimes lead to employees working long hours, neglecting self-care, and experiencing burnout. The relentless pursuit of high performance may result in a lack of work-life balance, which can negatively impact employee well-being and overall job satisfaction.
- The high expectations and performance standards in a high-performing culture can create a highly competitive and demanding work environment. This intense pressure can be mentally and emotionally taxing for employees, potentially leading to increased stress levels, anxiety, and even conflicts among team members.
- While high-performing cultures emphasise efficiency and achievement, they may inadvertently stifle innovation and risk-taking. The focus on meeting targets and maintaining high performance levels can discourage employees from taking innovative approaches or exploring unconventional ideas. This can limit the organisation's ability to adapt to changing market dynamics and it may potentially miss out on valuable opportunities.

- To maintain high levels of performance, leaders in high-performing cultures may resort to micromanagement. The desire for control and precision can result in limited autonomy and decision-making authority for employees. This can hinder their sense of ownership and empowerment, leading to decreased job satisfaction; employees may experience fatigue or complacency due to the constant pressure to perform at peak levels. This can lead to a decline in motivation, creativity, and overall performance.
- High-performing cultures may unintentionally create barriers to diversity and inclusion. The focus on performance metrics and achieving targets can overshadow the importance of creating a diverse and inclusive workforce. This can limit the perspectives and experiences brought to the table, potentially hindering innovation and limiting the organisation's ability to connect with diverse customer bases.
- In a high-performing culture, the pursuit of excellence and recognition can breed unhealthy competition among employees. Instead of fostering teamwork, it may create a culture where individuals prioritise personal success over collective achievements. This can undermine trust, collaboration, and the overall cohesiveness of the organisation.

It's crucial for organisations to be aware of these potential weaknesses and take proactive measures to address them. By fostering a supportive work environment, promoting work-life balance, encouraging risk-taking and creativity, nurturing diversity and inclusion, and maintaining open channels of communication, organisations can mitigate these weaknesses and build a more sustainable and resilient high-performing culture.

Opportunities

High-performing cultures present several opportunities for organisations to thrive and excel. By leveraging the strengths of these cultures, organisations can capitalise on various opportunities to drive success and achieve their goals. Opportunities related to high-performing cultures include:

- High-performing cultures prioritise productivity and efficiency, creating an opportunity for organisations to streamline processes, eliminate waste, and maximise output. Through effective performance management practices, organisations can optimise resource allocation, minimise redundancies, and improve overall operational effectiveness.
- High-performing cultures foster a mindset of continuous improvement and innovation. Employees are encouraged to seek better ways of doing things, challenge the status quo, and drive innovation within their respective roles. This presents an opportunity for organisations to stay ahead of the competition, adapt to changing market demands, and deliver cutting-edge products or services.
- A high-performing culture can provide a significant competitive advantage. Organisations with a track record of consistently achieving superior results and surpassing customer expectations are well positioned to differentiate themselves from competitors. This can lead to increased market share, customer loyalty, and a favourable brand reputation.
- High-performing cultures emphasise continuous learning and development. Organisations can leverage this opportunity by providing employees with the necessary resources, training, and mentorship to enhance their skills and knowledge. By investing in employee growth, organisations not only strengthen

their talent pool but also foster a culture of knowledge sharing and adaptability.

» High-performing cultures are often characterised by agility and adaptability. Employees are encouraged to embrace change, be resilient, and respond effectively to evolving market dynamics. This enables organisations to navigate uncertainties, seize emerging opportunities, and proactively address challenges.
» Organisations with high-performing cultures are more likely to deliver exceptional customer experiences. By consistently meeting or exceeding customer expectations, organisations can enhance customer satisfaction, build long-term relationships, and generate customer loyalty. Satisfied customers can become brand advocates and contribute to business growth through positive word-of-mouth and referrals.

By seizing these opportunities, organisations can cultivate a culture of high performance that drives success, fosters innovation, attracts top talent, and creates a sustainable competitive advantage. However, it's important for organisations to remain agile and adapt their high-performing culture to changing circumstances to capitalise on emerging opportunities and stay ahead in a rapidly evolving business landscape.

Threats

While high-performing cultures offer numerous benefits, it's essential to be aware of potential threats that can undermine their effectiveness and long-term success. Understanding these threats allows organisations to proactively address them and safeguard their high-performing culture. The following are some threats linked with high-performing cultures:

» A relentless pursuit of high performance can lead to excessive workloads, long hours, and high levels of stress among employees. If not managed effectively, this can result in burnout and work-life imbalance, negatively impacting employee well-being and overall productivity. Organisations must prioritise work-life balance, implement strategies to prevent burnout, and promote a healthy and sustainable work environment.

» High-performing cultures can sometimes inadvertently lead to a lack of diversity and inclusion. If the focus is solely on performance metrics without considering the importance of diversity in perspectives, backgrounds, and experiences, organisations risk creating similar environments that stifle innovation and hinder creativity. It's crucial to foster a culture that values and embraces diversity, ensuring equitable opportunities for all employees.

» High-performing cultures may become complacent and resistant to change if success breeds a sense of entitlement or a fear of disrupting what has been working well. Organisations must guard against complacency and encourage a growth mindset that embraces change and continuous improvement. By proactively seeking new ideas, challenging the status quo, and adapting to market dynamics, organisations can maintain their competitive edge.

» While healthy competition can drive performance, an overly competitive environment can create internal strife, a lack of collaboration, and a toxic work culture. When individuals prioritise personal achievements over collective goals, it can undermine teamwork, hinder knowledge sharing, and negatively impact overall organisational performance. Organisations should foster a culture of collaboration, teamwork, and shared success to mitigate the threats of unhealthy competition.

- Leadership plays a critical role in sustaining a high-performing culture. If there is a lack of effective leadership or a leadership vacuum, it can undermine the culture and create a sense of uncertainty and disengagement among employees. Organisations must invest in developing strong leaders who can inspire, empower, and align teams towards high performance.
- External factors such as economic downturns, technological advancements, or industry disruptions can pose threats to high-performing cultures. Organisations must stay vigilant, adapt to changing market conditions, and proactively address emerging challenges. By fostering resilience, agility, and a proactive approach to change, organisations can mitigate the impact of external threats on their high-performing culture.
- Recognition and rewards are essential to sustain a high-performing culture. If employees feel their efforts are not acknowledged or appropriately rewarded, it can lead to demotivation, decreased engagement, and attrition. Organisations should establish robust recognition and reward systems that celebrate individual and team achievements, fostering a culture of appreciation and motivation.

By acknowledging and addressing these threats, organisations can safeguard their high-performing culture, maintain employee well-being, and sustain long-term success. Regular evaluation, feedback mechanisms, and a commitment to continuous improvement are crucial in navigating potential threats and ensuring the longevity of a high-performing culture.

The key takeaways in this chapter include:

- A high-performing culture is an organisational environment where employees are motivated, empowered, and supported to consistently perform at their best, achieve their goals, and contribute to the overall success of the organisation. It prioritises excellence, continuous improvement, accountability, and results.

- A high-performing culture is aligned with the organisation's vision, values, and strategic objectives. It fosters collaboration, teamwork, and innovation. Leaders in a high-performing culture set high standards, provide support and guidance, and promote a positive and inclusive work environment.

- A high-performing culture is important because it drives organisational success. It leads to improved performance, increased productivity, employee engagement, customer satisfaction, talent attraction, and competitive advantage.

- Different types of high-performing cultures exist, including performance-driven culture, innovation and creativity culture, collaborative culture, customer-centric culture, learning and development culture, and ethical and values-driven culture. These types may coexist in organisations, depending on their values, goals, and industry.

- Signs of a high-performing culture include clarity and alignment around goals, individual and collective accountability, a focus on learning and growth, effective dialogue and teamwork, a culture of innovation, recognition and rewards, and a positive work environment.

- Creating a high-performing culture involves defining core values, modelling desired behaviours, fostering open conversations, providing resources and autonomy, recognising and rewarding performance, encouraging collaboration and innovation, and regularly assessing and adjusting the culture.

- Building a high-performing culture can face challenges like resistance to change, lack of alignment, and departmental silos. Solutions include strong leadership, effective communication, collaboration, learning programmes, and promoting a safe and supportive environment for continuous improvement.

- Sustaining a high-performing culture requires ongoing commitment and reinforcement. It involves embedding the desired values and behaviours into daily operations, nurturing a culture of continuous learning and improvement, and cultivating an environment that supports and empowers employees to sustain their high performance.

CHAPTER 4: Illuminating the "Shadow Culture" Impacting Organisations

Creating a high-performing culture can be an excellent way to help companies achieve great things. Over the years of being an employee, manager, leader, and HR professional I have continually encountered something beneath the surface. I have sensed a hidden element, an unspoken truth waiting to be unravelled, which I will refer to as a "shadow culture". I would describe it as an intricate tapestry that exists within organisational life, unveiling a concealed realm of beliefs, values, and behaviours that coexist alongside the official narrative of an organisation's mission statement, vision, and values.

These hidden cultures emerge through a complex interplay of factors such as power dynamics, resistance to change, misalignment between leadership and employees, and breakdowns in communication. They can manifest in various forms, each with its own distinct characteristics and impact on organisational well-being.

In this chapter, I will explore the types of shadow cultures that exist in organisations. I will shed light on these often-hidden cultures that can breed negativity and hinder collaboration, as well as stifle innovation and create silos within organisations. By recognising the signs that indicate the presence of a shadow culture, we can better understand the hidden dynamics that affect employee morale, engagement, and overall performance.

Moreover, I will examine how shadow cultures are created, recognising the crucial role played by leaders, organisational structures, communication patterns, and the treatment of employee well-being. Understanding the root causes and underlying mechanisms will allow us to address these issues effectively and embark on a journey of cultural transformation.

While shadow cultures are primarily associated with weaknesses and threats, I will also explore the potential strengths and opportunities they offer. By harnessing the resilience, innovation, and diversity of perspectives found within shadow cultures, organisations can channel these attributes towards positive change, fostering inclusive environments, collaboration, and adaptability.

So, let's now venture into the realm of shadow cultures, uncovering their complexities, and discovering how they shape the organisations we inhabit. Together, we will unravel the shadows and illuminate the path to a healthier and more vibrant organisational culture.

What is a shadow culture?

A shadow culture refers to a hidden or unofficial set of beliefs, values, and behaviours that exist within an organisation alongside its official or visible culture. This shadow culture often emerges because of unspoken norms, informal practices, and implicit attitudes that are contrary to the organisation's stated values and goals. It can manifest as a counterproductive or toxic subculture that undermines the desired organisational culture.

The shadow culture may arise due to various factors, such as power dynamics, resistance to change, lack of alignment between leadership and employees, or gaps in communication. It can perpetuate detrimental behaviours like gossip, mistrust, unethical conduct, or resistance to collaboration. The presence of a shadow culture can hinder organisational performance, impede teamwork, and create a negative work environment.

Identifying and addressing the shadow culture is crucial for cultivating a healthy and high-performing organisational culture. It requires open dialogue, transparency, and a commitment to aligning the hidden norms and behaviours with the desired values and goals of the organisation. By acknowledging and addressing the shadow culture, organisations can foster a culture that promotes trust, collaboration, and the overall well-being of its employees.

What type of shadow cultures exist in today's companies?

Various types of shadow cultures may exist, which are unofficial or hidden cultures that emerge within an organisation. These cultures often contrast with the organisation's formal or stated values and norms. While it's important to note that not all companies have shadow cultures, here are some examples of shadow cultures that can be found:

Toxic culture

This shadow culture often manifests in organisations where harmful behaviours are prevalent, such as bullying, harassment, or discrimination. It may stem from an underlying power dynamic or poor leadership, leading to a negative and unhealthy work environment.

Workaholic culture

Some companies develop a shadow culture that promotes an excessive focus on work and long working hours. This culture may place high expectations on employees to constantly be available and sacrifice personal well-being, leading to burnout and work-life imbalance.

Silo culture

In organisations with a silo culture, different departments or teams operate in isolation from one another, hindering collaboration and communication. This culture may result in a lack of information sharing, a reluctance to collaborate across teams, and a focus on the individual rather than collective success.

Political culture

In some companies, a shadow culture of office politics may emerge, where employees engage in manipulative or strategic behaviours to gain power or advance their own interests. This culture can lead to a competitive and cutthroat environment, fostering distrust and undermining teamwork.

Innovation-stifling culture

Companies that resist change and innovation may develop a shadow culture that discourages risk-taking and creative thinking. In such cultures, employees may be hesitant to propose new ideas or challenge existing processes due to a fear of failure or a lack of support for innovation.

Compliance culture

While compliance with regulations and policies is essential, a shadow culture may develop in organisations where an excessive focus on rules and procedures stifles autonomy and creativity. This culture may prioritise adherence to rules over outcomes, leading to a lack of flexibility and agility.

It's important for organisations to identify and address these shadow cultures to foster healthier and more inclusive work environments that align with their desired values and goals.

Signs of a shadow culture

Recognising the signs of a shadow culture within an organisation can be crucial for addressing any underlying issues and fostering a more positive work environment. Here are some signs that may indicate the presence of a shadow culture:

There is a **stark contrast** between the organisation's official mission, values, and policies and the behaviours, attitudes, and practices observed within the organisation.

Information is not readily shared, decisions are made behind closed doors, and there is a general atmosphere of **secrecy or selective disclosure**.

It is a **hierarchical structure** that promotes favouritism, unfair treatment, or the abuse of power. Individuals with authority may take advantage of their positions, and there may be a lack of accountability for their actions.

A significant number of employees leave the organisation or express **dissatisfaction and low motivation**, which can be

There is a ***stark contrast*** between the organisation's official mission, values, and policies and the behaviours, attitudes, and practices observed within the organisation.

indicative of an unhealthy or toxic work environment.

Departments or teams **operate in isolation**, and there is minimal interaction, knowledge sharing, or cooperation across different areas of the organisation.

Managers and teams are **resistant to new ideas, feedback, or improvements**. There may be a fear of taking risks or a preference for maintaining the status quo, hindering creativity and adaptability.

There are instances of **discrimination** based on factors such as gender, race, age, or other protected characteristics, as well as harassment, bullying, or a hostile work environment.

There is an environment that **fosters cutthroat competition** among employees or teams, with limited collaboration, support, or recognition of shared goals.

Rules, regulations, or policies are **inconsistently applied**, leading to perceptions of favouritism or unfair treatment.

Employees display signs of stress, burnout, anxiety, or other **negative effects on their mental or physical health** due to work-related factors.

It's important to note that these signs do not necessarily guarantee the existence of a shadow culture, but they can serve as indicators for further investigation or evaluation of the organisational culture and its impact on employees.

How shadow cultures are created

Shadow cultures within companies can be created through various factors and circumstances. Here are some ways in which shadow cultures may emerge:

The behaviour and actions of leaders and managers play a significant role in shaping organisational culture. If leaders exhibit poor leadership skills, favouritism, or unethical behaviour, it can set the tone for a shadow culture to develop. Inconsistent enforcement of policies, lack of accountability, or failure to address toxic behaviour can contribute to the formation of a shadow culture.

Organisational structure and communication can inadvertently create silos or barriers to effective communication and collaboration. When departments or teams work in isolation with limited interaction, it can foster a shadow culture of secrecy, competition, and information hoarding.

When companies go through mergers or acquisitions, the blending of different organisational cultures can create conflicts or tension. If the integration process is mishandled or cultural differences are not properly addressed, it can lead to the emergence of a shadow culture that undermines collaboration and unity.

Organisations that lack diversity and fail to foster an inclusive environment may inadvertently create a shadow culture that marginalises certain groups or perpetuates biases.

If leaders exhibit poor leadership skills, favouritism, or unethical behaviour, it can set the tone for a shadow culture to develop.

Discrimination, exclusionary practices, or unconscious biases can contribute to the formation of a toxic or exclusive culture within the organisation.

Neglecting employee well-being and prioritising productivity and profitability over employee well-being can inadvertently create a shadow culture that promotes overwork, stress, and burnout. When employees' physical and emotional health is not prioritised, it can lead to a culture of constant pressure, low morale, and disengagement.

If an organisation's stated values and mission are not consistently reinforced through actions and decisions, employees may perceive a disconnect between what is officially communicated and what is practised. This discrepancy can erode trust and contribute to the formation of a shadow culture that goes against the desired values.

When employees feel that their voices are not heard or that there are limited opportunities for open and honest communication, it can foster an environment where concerns or dissenting opinions are suppressed. This can lead to the development of a shadow culture where important issues remain unaddressed and dissatisfaction festers.

It's important to note that shadow cultures can emerge gradually and may result from a combination of factors. Organisations should actively promote a positive and inclusive culture, prioritise effective leadership, encourage open communication, and regularly assess and address any signs of a potential shadow culture.

Overall impact of shadow culture

Strengths

- Often this type of culture develops as a response to challenging or adverse conditions within an organisation. The individuals within these cultures have developed resilience and adaptability to navigate and survive in such environments.
- Within a shadow culture, diverse perspectives and unconventional thinking can flourish. This can lead to the emergence of innovative ideas and approaches that challenge the status quo and drive positive change.
- Individuals within shadow cultures often develop resourcefulness as they find ways to navigate complex power dynamics and overcome obstacles. This resourcefulness can contribute to problem-solving skills and creative solutions.
- Shadow cultures provide a different lens through which to view an organisation. They bring attention to the discrepancies between the stated values and the actual behaviours and practices within the organisation, enabling a deeper understanding of the organisational dynamics.
- Informal networks and knowledge sharing among employees who share common experiences and challenges can be created organically. These networks can facilitate knowledge sharing, mentoring, and support, creating pockets of expertise within the organisation.
- This type of culture can bring together individuals with diverse backgrounds, experiences, and viewpoints. This diversity of perspectives can lead to more comprehensive problem-solving, increased creativity, and a broader range of solutions.

- Recognising the presence of a shadow culture can serve as a catalyst for positive change within an organisation. By acknowledging and addressing the underlying issues, organisations can transform their culture, improve employee morale, and drive performance and innovation.

It's important to note that while these strengths exist within a shadow culture, they often come with significant drawbacks and potential negative consequences. Harnessing these strengths in a productive manner requires a careful assessment of the underlying issues, active efforts to address systemic challenges, and alignment with the organisation's formal values and goals.

Weaknesses

- Shadow cultures often emerge as a result of misalignment between the official culture and the hidden norms and behaviours within an organisation. This lack of alignment can lead to confusion, inconsistency, and a loss of focus on shared goals and values.
- Negative work environments, particularly toxic or dysfunctional ones, create a negative work environment characterised by gossip, mistrust, and unethical behaviour. This toxic atmosphere can erode employee morale, lead to high turnover rates, and hinder productivity and collaboration.
- This culture can promote a siloed mindset, where different departments or teams operate in isolation, hindering effective communication, information sharing, and collaboration. This lack of cross-functional collaboration can impede efficiency and innovation.
- Resistance to change can be a side effect of a shadow culture, often due to a fear of failure or a preference for maintaining the status quo. This resistance can stifle creativity, prevent the adoption of new ideas, and

hinder the organisation's ability to adapt to evolving market demands.

- In shadow cultures, there may be a lack of accountability for inappropriate behaviour, favouritism, or abuses of power. This lack of accountability can undermine trust and fairness within the organisation, leading to disengagement and a negative impact on overall performance.
- Shadow cultures often discourage open and honest communication, making it difficult for employees to provide feedback, express concerns, or voice dissenting opinions. This lack of communication channels can perpetuate issues and prevent constructive dialogue and problem-solving.
- Some shadow cultures may marginalise certain groups or perpetuate biases, leading to discrimination, unequal treatment, and a lack of diversity and inclusion. This exclusionary environment can limit the organisation's ability to leverage the full potential of its workforce and hinder innovation and collaboration.

It is essential for organisations to recognise these weaknesses and take proactive measures to address and rectify any shadow cultures that may exist. This involves promoting a positive and inclusive organisational culture, establishing clear values and expectations, fostering open communication, and providing avenues for feedback and accountability.

Opportunities

- Shadow cultures often contain untapped potential in terms of skills, knowledge, and innovative thinking. By recognising and leveraging this potential, organisations can harness the strengths and talents within shadow cultures to drive positive change and improve overall performance.

- These cultures may represent diverse perspectives, backgrounds, and experiences that are not fully integrated into the official organisational culture. Embracing and incorporating these diverse viewpoints can promote inclusivity, enhance creativity, and foster a more representative and equitable work environment.
- Addressing and transforming shadow cultures can significantly improve employee engagement. By creating a culture of transparency, open communication, and trust, organisations can foster a sense of belonging and purpose among employees, leading to higher levels of motivation, commitment, and productivity.
- Shadow cultures often offer opportunities for learning and personal development. By encouraging knowledge sharing, mentorship, and collaboration within these cultures, organisations can create a dynamic learning environment that promotes continuous growth and professional advancement.
- They can be a source of innovative thinking and a catalyst for change. By embracing diverse perspectives and alternative ideas within shadow cultures, organisations can foster a culture of innovation, adaptability, and continuous improvement.
- This type of culture can provide insights into the underlying challenges and weaknesses within an organisation. By addressing and transforming these cultures, organisations can enhance their resilience to external disruptions, improve problem-solving capabilities, and better navigate change and uncertainty.
- Recognising and addressing shadow cultures provides an opportunity for cultural transformation. By aligning the hidden norms and behaviours with the desired values and goals of the organisation, organisations can cultivate a healthier, more inclusive, and high-performing

culture that supports the well-being and success of its employees.

It's important to note that these opportunities can only be realised through deliberate efforts to address and transform the shadow culture into a positive and aligned organisational culture. This requires a commitment from leadership, active engagement from employees, and ongoing evaluation and reinforcement of the desired culture.

Threats

- Shadow cultures that perpetuate toxic behaviours, unethical conduct, or discrimination can significantly damage an organisation's reputation. Negative experiences and perceptions shared by employees or other stakeholders can tarnish the organisation's image and hinder its ability to attract and retain top talent.
- They can foster a negative work environment, lack of collaboration, or resistance to change which can lead to decreased productivity and performance. Employees may become disengaged, demotivated, and less willing to contribute their best efforts, resulting in reduced overall organisational effectiveness.
- Toxic shadow cultures can contribute to high employee turnover rates as individuals seek better work environments and opportunities elsewhere. Losing valuable talent due to a negative culture can disrupt operations, increase recruitment costs, and lead to a loss of institutional knowledge and expertise.
- Legal and compliance risks that involve discriminatory practices, harassment, or other unethical behaviours pose legal and compliance risks for organisations. Violations of laws and regulations can result in legal

consequences, lawsuits, financial penalties, and damage to the organisation's reputation.

- » Shadow cultures that resist change and discourage innovation can hinder an organisation's ability to adapt to evolving market demands and stay competitive. The absence of a culture that encourages new ideas and creative thinking can lead to stagnation and missed opportunities for growth and improvement.
- » These cultures that perpetuate stress, burnout, and a lack of work-life balance can have detrimental effects on employee well-being. This can result in decreased mental and physical health, increased absenteeism, and reduced overall employee satisfaction.
- » Shadow cultures that promote silos, limited information sharing, or a lack of collaboration can hinder effective communication and teamwork. This can lead to misalignment, duplication of efforts, and decreased efficiency and productivity across departments and teams.

Shadow cultures can severely harm an organisation's reputation, leading to decreased productivity, disengaged employees, and high turnover rates. Legal risks from discriminatory practices and non-compliance can result in financial penalties and lawsuits. These cultures hinder innovation and adaptability, affecting competitiveness. Additionally, they impact employee well-being, leading to burnout, absenteeism, and reduced satisfaction. Limited collaboration and communication further hamper efficiency and productivity.

The key takeaways in this chapter include:

» Shadow culture refers to the hidden beliefs, values, and behaviours that exist within an organisation alongside its official culture. It represents the unseen realm where informal practices, implicit attitudes, and unspoken rules shape the experiences of employees and the overall functioning of the organisation.

» This culture can emerge from a combination of factors such as power dynamics, resistance to change, misalignment between leadership and employees, and breakdowns in communication. Understanding their diverse manifestations is crucial to addressing their impact on organisational well-being.

» Toxic shadow cultures breed negativity and hinder collaboration within an organisation. They create a hostile environment, eroding employee morale, engagement, and overall performance.

» Siloed cultures form within organisations, hindering communication, collaboration, and innovation. They impede the organisation's ability to adapt and thrive in a rapidly changing environment.

» The creation of shadow cultures involves examining the role of leaders, organisational structures, communication patterns, and employee well-being. Identifying the root causes and underlying mechanisms enables organisations to effectively address these issues and embark on cultural transformation.

» The strengths and opportunities of shadow cultures can offer the potential for resilience, innovation, and diversity of perspectives. By harnessing these strengths, organisations can drive positive change and create inclusive environments.

» Recognising signs of a shadow culture is crucial for aligning formal and informal cultures. Bringing hidden dynamics to light enables organisations to foster thriving environments where collaboration flourishes and desired values are embodied.

» Addressing shadow cultures requires a commitment to open dialogue, transparency, and inclusivity. Organisations must create safe spaces for employees to voice their experiences, challenge existing norms, and actively participate in shaping a more authentic and aligned organisational culture.

CHAPTER 5: Food for Thought – Shadow Culture Case Studies

In this chapter, I delve into three case studies that shed light on the detrimental effects of shadow cultures within different organisations and their impact on integrity and trust. We will explore the Metropolitan Police Service (Met), the Partygate scandal, and the Post Office scandal, examining why these case studies were chosen, the specific issues they highlight, and the valuable lessons that can be learned from each.

The reason I have put these case studies in here is firstly, the case studies highlight the pressing need for organisations to acknowledge and actively address shadow cultures. They reveal the severe consequences of allowing toxic cultures to persist, including institutionalised discrimination, abuse, and a lack of accountability.

Secondly, reviewing real case studies can help us understand that addressing shadow cultures requires more than lip service. It necessitates a genuine commitment to transparency, effective communication, ethical leadership, and a culture of accountability. Lastly, by learning from these past mistakes and actively dismantling toxic cultures, organisations can foster inclusive and supportive environments, rebuild trust, and pave the way for long-term success.

By studying these case studies, we can gain insight into the complex nature of shadow cultures and the importance of actively challenging and transforming them. By doing so, organisations can create spaces that encourage diversity of thought, foster open communication, and promote a culture of respect and inclusivity.

> *Disclaimer: The following three case studies are based on my own interpretation of available information, and their complexity may not be fully captured. They are presented solely to illustrate how a neglected shadow culture can escalate into significant issues.*

Case study: Metropolitan Police Service[6]

The March 2023 publication of the Baroness Casey Review on the Metropolitan Police Service (Met) shed light on a shadow culture of dysfunction within the organisation. Despite the commendable efforts of many police officers, the review reveals the presence of institutional racism, sexism, and homophobia.

At the core of the issue lies inadequate management characterised by disjointed initiatives, a lack of clear goals and strategies, and outdated workforce planning. Flawed recruitment and vetting processes allow individuals with predatory and bullying tendencies to enter the organisation. The absence of central training records results in officers being ill-prepared for their assigned roles, contributing to subpar performance.

The demanding nature of police work exacerbates the situation, placing immense pressure on officers managing junior staff without adequate resources. This environment tolerates or dismisses discriminatory acts, perpetuating a culture that undermines trust. The review calls for tangible actions from the Met to regain public trust beyond mere rhetoric.

This case study underscores the detrimental effects of a toxic organisation culture and emphasises the importance of effective leadership, robust management systems, and a commitment to diversity, equality, and inclusion. Addressing and rectifying toxic cultures can create a positive and accountable work environment, fostering trust and confidence among stakeholders for long-term success.

Case study: The Partygate scandal[7]

The Partygate scandal unfolded during the COVID-19 pandemic in 2020 and 2021, shaking the UK's political landscape. It involved a series of parties and gatherings held by government and Conservative Party staff, blatantly disregarding public health restrictions. These events played a significant role in the downfall of Prime Minister Boris Johnson.

Despite the implementation of multiple lockdowns and strict regulations, numerous gatherings took place at 10 Downing Street, in government buildings, and the garden. As news of these gatherings emerged, they captured the attention of the media, sparked public outrage, and ignited political controversy. In January 2022, an investigation was launched into 12 of these events, some of which had been attended by Prime Minister Johnson himself. As a result, 126 fixed penalty notices were issued to 83 individuals, including the Prime Minister, his wife, and the then Chancellor of the Exchequer, all of whom apologised and paid the penalties.

The scandal initially came to light when the *Daily Mirror* reported on staff gatherings at 10 Downing Street during the Christmas season of 2020. Downing Street initially denied the existence of any parties, but a leaked video of a mock press conference revealed joking references to such gatherings. The fallout from this revelation led to the resignation of Downing Street's press secretary at the time. Subsequent reports disclosed additional events, including a gathering in the garden during the first national lockdown and two events on the day before Prince Philip's funeral. The scandal also implicated Conservative Party staff gatherings held to celebrate the Prime Minister's birthday in June 2020.

In response to the leaked video, the Cabinet Office launched an inquiry led by civil servant Sue Gray. However, the investigation faced delays due to the concurrent Metropolitan Police investigation into potential breaches of COVID-19 regulations. In May 2022, Gray's final report unveiled a pattern of excessive drinking and a lack of respect for cleaning and security staff across multiple events. She concluded that senior political and civil service leaders must take responsibility for cultivating such a culture.

The scandal's impact reverberated with the public, leading to a decline in support for Prime Minister Johnson, the government, and the Conservative Party. Calls for Johnson's resignation or a vote of no confidence came from both opposition parties and a handful of Conservative politicians. Consequently, several senior Downing Street staff members resigned, and the allegations of Johnson misleading Parliament were referred to the Parliamentary Privileges Committee.

Ultimately, the Partygate scandal served as a turning point, shifting public sentiment, and underscoring the dire need for accountability and integrity in political leadership. It stands as a cautionary tale, reminding us of the consequences that arise when a shadow culture takes hold, jeopardising the well-being of individuals and eroding the foundations of a democratic society.

Case study: The Post Office scandal[8]

The Horizon Scandal refers to a long-standing issue involving the Horizon accounting system, which aimed to automate financial transactions and network operations at Post Office branches. However, alongside the technical failures, another significant factor in the scandal was the existence of a shadow culture within the Post Office. This case study examines the background, impact, shadow culture, and subsequent inquiry surrounding the Horizon Scandal.

In 1997, the Post Office and the Department for Social Security (DSS) piloted the Horizon accounting system to automate financial transactions and migrate benefits at Post Office branches. However, the system's flaws became evident in 2000 when errors started to occur, resulting in substantial shortfalls in individual branch accounts.

Between 2000 and 2014, the Post Office prosecuted 736 sub-postmasters and sub-postmistresses based on information provided by the Horizon computer system. These prosecutions, averaging one per week, led to convictions for false accounting and theft, resulting in imprisonment for some individuals. Many innocent sub-postmasters faced financial ruin, while others experienced social isolation as their communities shunned them. Tragically, some victims of the scandal have since passed away.

The Horizon Scandal highlighted the existence of a shadow culture within the Post Office. This shadow culture was characterised by a lack of transparency, top-down pressure, and a dismissive attitude towards sub-postmasters who raised concerns about the system's inaccuracies. Rather than acknowledging and addressing the problems with the Horizon system, the Post Office chose to prosecute sub-postmasters, compounding the impact on their lives and perpetuating a culture of fear and mistrust.

Due to the severity of the situation and persistent campaigning by parliamentarians, an independent inquiry into the Horizon Scandal was promised by Prime Minister Boris Johnson on 26 February 2020. The inquiry, led by Sir Wyn Williams, commenced as a non-statutory investigation in Autumn 2020, with its scope outlined in September 2020. However, the Justice For Subpostmasters Alliance (JFSA) refused to participate in the inquiry, considering it to be a "whitewash", and called for a full public inquiry instead.

In response to demands for a more comprehensive investigation, the government announced on 19 May 2021 that the Horizon Scandal inquiry would become a statutory inquiry. This change meant that witnesses could be compelled to give evidence. The decision came after convictions were quashed and it was anticipated that many more would follow. In November 2021, Sir Wyn issued a press release outlining the issues to be considered by the inquiry, including the shadow culture within the Post Office and its impact on the treatment of sub-postmasters.

The Horizon Scandal, exacerbated by the existence of a shadow culture within the Post Office, has had profound consequences for sub-postmasters and sub-postmistresses. The flawed implementation of the Horizon accounting system, coupled with a lack of transparency and accountability, resulted in financial and personal hardships for innocent individuals. The ongoing statutory inquiry seeks to uncover the truth, examine compensation schemes, and address the issue of the shadow culture. It is hoped that this inquiry will bring about systemic changes, fostering a culture of openness, fairness, and accountability within the Post Office and preventing such injustices from occurring in the future.

What can we learn from these case studies?

The revelations surrounding the Partygate scandal provide a striking example of a toxic shadow culture within a prominent political party. This culture of illicit behaviour and unethical practices, fostered by privilege, entitlement, and a failure of leadership, compromised the integrity and trust the organisation aimed to uphold. It underscores the critical importance of transparency, accountability, and ethical leadership in maintaining institutional integrity.

The Baroness Casey Review of the Metropolitan Police Service further highlighted the presence of a dysfunctional and toxic culture within the organisation. This culture was rife with institutional racism, sexism, and homophobia, necessitating urgent reforms in leadership and management systems, and a commitment to diversity, equality, and inclusion. Rectifying such toxic cultures is crucial to create a positive work environment, rebuilding trust, and paving the way for long-term success.

Additionally, the Post Office scandal exposed a shadow culture driven by unrealistic targets and profitability. This toxic environment resulted in wrongful prosecutions and severe consequences for innocent individuals. Lack of transparency, effective communication, and a blame-and-punishment culture perpetuated this shadow culture, emphasising the need for organisations to prioritise transparency, communication, and a culture of accountability.

Collectively, these case studies underscore the pressing need for organisations to acknowledge and actively address shadow cultures. Failing to address such cultures can lead to institutionalised discrimination, abuse, and a lack of accountability. Building inclusive and supportive work environments is vital for organisations to rebuild trust, protect individuals, and ensure long-term success.

It is crucial for organisations to understand that addressing shadow cultures goes beyond rhetoric. It requires a genuine commitment to transparency, effective communication, ethical leadership, and a culture of accountability. By learning from past mistakes and actively dismantling toxic cultures, organisations can foster inclusive and supportive environments where all individuals can thrive and contribute to overall success.

In summary, these case studies provide valuable insights, reminding us of the paramount importance of nurturing a healthy organisational culture rooted in trust, transparency, and ethical practices. Only by actively addressing and rectifying shadow cultures can organisations fulfil their potential and regain the trust and confidence of stakeholders.

The key takeaways in this chapter include:

- The case studies highlight the urgent need for organisations to address shadow cultures. Ignoring such cultures can lead to severe consequences, including institutional discrimination, abuse, and a lack of accountability.

- Real case studies emphasise that addressing shadow cultures requires more than lip service; it necessitates genuine commitment to transparency, effective communication, ethical leadership, and a culture of accountability.

- By actively dismantling toxic cultures, organisations can foster inclusive and supportive environments, rebuild trust, and pave the way for long-term success.

- Toxic shadow cultures can lead to a negative work environment, lack of collaboration, resistance to change, decreased productivity, and employee disengagement.

- High employee turnover rates can result from toxic shadow cultures, leading to operational disruptions, increased recruitment costs, and loss of institutional knowledge and expertise.

- Legal and compliance risks arise from discriminatory practices, harassment, and unethical behaviours within shadow cultures, leading to legal consequences, financial penalties, and damage to the organisation's reputation.

- Shadow cultures that resist change and discourage innovation can hinder an organisation's adaptability and competitiveness, leading to stagnation and missed growth opportunities.

- Toxic shadow cultures perpetuate stress, burnout, and a lack of work-life balance, adversely affecting employee well-being, mental and physical health, and overall satisfaction.

- Shadow cultures that promote silos and limited collaboration hinder effective communication and teamwork, leading to misalignment, duplication of efforts, and decreased efficiency and productivity across departments and teams.

CHAPTER 6: Shaping Positive Change – Conclusion

Organisation culture plays a pivotal role in shaping the environment and success of an organisation. It encompasses shared values, beliefs, attitudes, behaviours, and practices that define how employees interact with one another, approach their work, and engage with customers. Understanding the factors that influence an individual's socialisation, such as family, peers, schools, media, and work, provides insights into the formation of organisation culture.

Leaders have a significant impact on shaping organisation culture through their leadership style, values, attitudes, and decision-making. Organisation values and mission statements act as guiding principles, providing a sense of direction and purpose for employees. The structure of an organisation, including its hierarchy and communication channels, as well as the physical environment of the workplace, contribute to shaping the culture.

Diversity and inclusivity within an organisation foster a culture of innovation and collaboration, contributing to the organisation's overall success. Rituals, traditions, and ceremonies reinforce values and create a sense of belonging among employees. External factors, such as industry trends and market conditions, can also influence an organisation's culture.

A high-performing culture, characterised by motivated, empowered, and supported employees, is crucial for driving organisational success. It prioritises excellence, continuous improvement, accountability, and results, aligning with the organisation's vision, values, and strategic objectives. Different types of high-performing cultures may coexist within organisations, depending on their values, goals, and industry.

Creating and maintaining a high-performing culture involves defining core values, modelling desired behaviours, fostering open communication, providing resources and autonomy, recognising and rewarding performance, encouraging collaboration and innovation, and regularly assessing and adjusting the culture.

However, alongside the official culture, there exists a shadow culture – an unseen realm of hidden beliefs, values, and behaviours within an organisation. Shadow cultures can have both positive and negative impacts on an organisation. Toxic shadow cultures breed negativity and hinder collaboration, while siloed cultures impede communication and innovation.

By unravelling the shadows and illuminating the path to a healthier organisational culture, organisations can create spaces that promote employee well-being, engagement, and long-term success.

It is essential for organisations to recognise the signs of a shadow culture and align their formal and informal cultures to foster environments where employees thrive, collaboration flourishes, and desired values are embodied. By harnessing the strengths and opportunities within shadow cultures, organisations can drive positive change and create inclusive environments.

A strong and positive organisation culture, coupled with an awareness and understanding of shadow cultures, can unleash the full potential of an organisation. Building a high-performing culture while addressing shadow cultures requires ongoing effort, collaboration, and a commitment to continuous improvement. Ultimately, organisations that prioritise culture and actively work towards its development are more likely to thrive in today's dynamic and competitive business world.

PART 2: How to Change Organisational Cultures

In today's ever-changing business world, creating a strong organisational culture is a vital ingredient for success. As discussed in Part 1 of this book, culture helps shape the identity, values, and beliefs of our organisations and can significantly impact employee engagement, productivity and, ultimately, the bottom line.

Although going on a transformational journey can reduce the presence of shadow cultures within organisations, the path to cultural change may not be easy or immediate. It may feel like a daunting task that requires significant effort, time, and resources.

However, the potential benefits are profound. By actively addressing and rectifying toxic behaviours and hidden practices, organisations can create a culture of transparency, accountability, and ethical leadership. This intentional effort to reduce the shadow culture fosters an environment where trust flourishes, employee well-being is prioritised, and collaboration and innovation thrive.

With a collective commitment to nurturing a healthy and inclusive organisation culture, organisations can cultivate an environment that embraces diversity, empowers employees, and values integrity. By creating a hopeful vision for the future, an organisation can also make a positive impact on partners, stakeholders, and society. And this is where this section of the book has been designed to help you.

Here, you will discover a wealth of valuable insights and practical tools aimed at cultivating a culture that not only fuels success but also nurtures employee satisfaction. With a focus on empowering individuals at every level, this section provides guidance on how to create a culture that thrives on transparency, accountability, and continuous improvement.

However, before we jump into my model for changing culture, let's briefly recap on a few points covered in Part 1, about the impact of leadership on culture and the role of communication in driving cultural change.

Leadership plays a crucial role in shaping and maintaining your organisation's culture. The leaders of your organisation are responsible for setting the tone and modelling the behaviours that will help define your culture. They therefore must articulate the values and beliefs of the organisation and ensure that these are reflected in every aspect of the organisation, from hiring and training to decision-making and communication. Leaders must also hold themselves and others accountable for living up to these values and demonstrating the desired behaviours. When leaders lead by example, they inspire and motivate others to do the same, creating a positive culture that is aligned with the organisation's goals and values.

In addition, effective communication is essential for driving cultural change in an organisation. To change the culture, employees need to understand the desired changes and why they are necessary. Leaders must communicate clearly and consistently about the new culture, its values, and its goals. This includes not only verbal communication but also non-verbal communication, such as the design of the physical environment or the way in which work is organised. Leaders must also listen to feedback from employees, customers, and other stakeholders to ensure that the change effort stays on track and remains responsive to evolving needs.

Effective communication can create a shared sense of purpose and commitment to the new culture, making it easier to overcome resistance and obstacles along the way. By creating a culture of open communication, companies can foster innovation, collaboration, and continuous improvement, leading to greater success and employee satisfaction.

The six-step Cultural Change Programme

In the following chapters, I share my Cultural Change model and, so you can see how it works in practice, you will be able to read a real-life case study in Chapter 14. I created this process because I believe companies require a methodical and well-structured approach to cultural change that facilitates an understanding of their existing culture, identifies areas that need improvement, and devises innovative solutions to drive change.

This model has been designed to help us change company cultures one step at a time, ultimately reducing the shadow cultures in our workplaces. However, I often hear a common concern when it comes to initiating change: "We simply don't have the time for this, we're too busy." I understand this sentiment all too well, having experienced it myself. That's why, before diving into the model, I'd like to propose an intriguing possibility: the introduction of a "shadow hunter" role within your company. In the next chapter, we will delve deeper into this concept and explore its potential impact.

The six-step Cultural Change Programme provides a framework for organisations to achieve the goal of transforming their culture, and in this introduction, we will explore each step in turn that can help your organisation build a stronger, more adaptable, and resilient culture.

Step One – Collaborative Commitment: This first step is about involving stakeholders at the outset and ensuring a shared vision for cultural change is created, building ownership and commitment to the process.

Step Two – Cultural Compass: Next I will show you how to conduct a thorough analysis of your organisation's current culture. Identifying areas for improvement will be covered in this step.

Step Three – Continuous Feedback: In this section, I will talk about the importance of gathering regular feedback from employees, customers, and other stakeholders and how this can help ensure that your cultural change efforts stay on track and responsive to evolving needs.

Step Four – Creative Concepts: By drawing on best practices and creative thinking, this section will help you develop tailored solutions that address your organisation's specific cultural challenges.

Step Five – Coordinated Execution: Here I will explore key elements to developing a detailed plan for implementing cultural change, and engaging employees in the process, to help ensure that your change efforts are successful and sustainable.

Step Six – Constant Assessment: Regularly evaluating progress and embedding cultural change into the fabric of the organisation is a step many people forget or skip so this will be covered in the last stage to help us ensure that the new culture becomes deeply ingrained and long-lasting.

The six-step Cultural Change Programme

CHAPTER 7: Exploring the Role of Shadow Hunters

Having delved into the realm of "shadow culture" in the first section of this book, I would now like to explore the idea of introducing a new role into organisations, either in an isolated role, integrated into other roles, or by using consultants or other specialists. This new role I will refer to as "shadow hunters". In this chapter, we will explore the significance of these individuals or groups who actively seek out and bring to light the hidden dimensions of the shadow culture present within organisations.

Shadow hunters assume a vital role in unravelling the intricacies of the shadow culture by diligently identifying and addressing informal practices, implicit attitudes, and unspoken rules that coexist alongside the official culture. Their commitment lies in comprehending the underlying mechanisms, root causes, and the impact of these concealed elements on the overall well-being of the organisation.

To shed light on the shadow culture, shadow hunters engage in various activities such as conducting interviews, facilitating focus groups, observing interactions, and gathering relevant data. Through collaboration with leaders, employees, and stakeholders, they strive to raise awareness, address toxic elements, dismantle silos, and cultivate a healthier and more inclusive work environment.

In essence, shadow hunters play a pivotal role in exposing and transforming the hidden aspects of an organisation's culture, thereby contributing to the enhancement of the overall organisational climate and the experiences of its employees.

To delve into this role, I have created a draft job description by way of an example. Please note that this example is intended to provide us with an understanding of the position and assess whether you believe it could align with your current or future organisational needs.

The role of shadow hunters – example job description

Draft job description

Purpose of role

Shadow hunters play a crucial role in identifying and addressing the hidden aspects of our organisational culture, with the aim of fostering positive change, transparency, and alignment between formal and informal elements.

Objective of the role

The primary objective of shadow hunters is to unravel the dynamics of the shadow culture, including informal practices, implicit attitudes, and unspoken rules that exist alongside the official culture.

Key areas of responsibility

- Engage in activities such as conducting interviews, organising focus groups, observing interactions, and gathering data to gain valuable insights into the shadow culture.
- Collaborate with leaders, employees, and other stakeholders to promote awareness, address toxic elements, break down silos, and create a healthier and more inclusive work environment.
- Aim to facilitate positive change by shedding light on the shadow culture, raising awareness, and working towards aligning the formal and informal aspects of our organisational culture.
- Responsible for actively seeking out and identifying hidden elements of the shadow culture that may impact organisational well-being.
- Analyse and understand the underlying mechanisms, root causes, and the impact of the shadow culture on our organisation.
- Responsible for gathering relevant data through interviews, surveys, observations, and other methods to gain insights into the shadow culture.
- Collaborate with leaders, employees, and other stakeholders to communicate their findings, promote awareness, and foster a culture of transparency and inclusion.
- Advocate for positive change by addressing toxic elements, recommending interventions, and supporting initiatives that align the formal and informal aspects of our organisational culture.
- Accountable for the accuracy and integrity of the data they collect and the insights they provide.
- Report findings, progress, and recommendations to relevant stakeholders, including leadership and the designated authority overseeing organisation culture.

» Regular progress updates and reports to be provided to ensure transparency and track the impact of shadow hunters' efforts on the organisation's culture.

Support and resources

The organisation will provide necessary support and resources to enable shadow hunters to fulfil their responsibilities effectively, including access to relevant information, training, and tools.

Shadow hunters will have the opportunity to collaborate and share best practices with other shadow hunters within the organisation to enhance their effectiveness and impact.

Collaborating with leaders and stakeholders

Collaborating with leaders and stakeholders is a fundamental aspect of the role of shadow hunters. By engaging with key individuals and groups within the organisation, shadow hunters can effectively address the hidden aspects of the shadow culture and drive positive change.

Shadow hunters actively establish and nurture relationships with leaders and stakeholders. They cultivate trust and rapport to foster open communication and create a supportive environment for addressing cultural challenges.

They proactively seek input from leaders and stakeholders regarding their observations and insights into the shadow culture. They value diverse perspectives and encourage an inclusive dialogue to gain a comprehensive understanding of the cultural dynamics.

They collaborate with leaders and stakeholders to communicate their findings regarding the informal practices, implicit attitudes, and unspoken rules that exist alongside the official culture. They present their insights in a clear and compelling manner, highlighting the potential impact on organisational well-being.

They work together with leaders and stakeholders to raise awareness about the shadow culture and its implications. They engage in discussions, workshops, and training sessions to foster a shared understanding and commitment to addressing cultural challenges.

They collaborate closely with leaders and stakeholders to identify and address toxic elements within the shadow culture. They facilitate discussions on strategies for eliminating harmful practices, promoting a healthy work environment, and fostering inclusivity and respect.

They also encourage collaboration and the breakdown of silos by facilitating cross-functional initiatives and fostering a culture of collaboration. They work with leaders and stakeholders to promote teamwork, knowledge sharing, and the dismantling of barriers that hinder effective communication and collaboration.

Shadow hunters collaborate with leaders and stakeholders to bridge the gap between the formal and informal aspects of the organisational culture. They assist in aligning policies, procedures, and values with the observed informal practices to create a cohesive culture that reflects the desired organisational values.

By collaborating with leaders and stakeholders, shadow hunters leverage collective expertise and influence to create a positive and inclusive work environment. This collaboration ensures that the efforts to address the shadow culture are integrated into the broader organisational strategy and that meaningful change is achieved throughout the organisation.

Overall impact of shadow hunter role

Strengths

Having a shadow hunter role in an organisation offers several strengths and benefits. Here are some of the key strengths:

Shadow hunters can bring a **heightened level of cultural awareness** to an organisation. They are attuned to the informal practices, implicit attitudes, and unspoken rules that exist alongside the official culture. By understanding these hidden aspects, shadow hunters can provide valuable insights into the dynamics of the organisation's culture.

They can actively seek out and **identify toxic elements**, cultural barriers, and areas of improvement that may go unnoticed by others. Their ability to shine a light on these issues can help an organisation address them effectively.

By exposing the shadow culture, shadow hunters **promote transparency and alignment** within the organisation. They bridge the gap between the formal and informal aspects of the culture, ensuring that there is consistency between what is officially stated and what is practised. This alignment fosters trust, engagement, and a more cohesive organisational culture.

They are attuned to the informal practices, implicit attitudes, and unspoken rules that exist alongside the official culture.

They **facilitate positive change** within the organisation, by addressing toxic elements, breaking down silos, and advocating for inclusivity. They can create a healthier work environment that encourages collaboration, innovation, and employee well-being. Their efforts contribute to a positive and thriving organisational culture.

Shadow hunters **gather valuable data** through interviews, observations, and other research methods. This data provides evidence-based insights into the shadow culture and its impact on the organisation. These insights help leaders make informed decisions and develop targeted interventions to improve the overall culture and employee experiences.

They collaborate closely with leaders, employees, and stakeholders throughout their work. They actively engage these key individuals and groups in conversations, workshops, and initiatives aimed at addressing cultural challenges. This collaboration fosters a **sense of ownership** and collective responsibility for cultural transformation.

Having a shadow hunter role encourages **continuous learning and growth** within the organisation. Shadow hunters bring new perspectives, knowledge, and best practices to the table. They promote a culture of curiosity, feedback, and continuous improvement, creating an environment where the organisation can evolve and adapt to changing circumstances.

By leveraging the strengths of a shadow hunter role, organisations can proactively address cultural issues, promote inclusivity, and create a positive and thriving work environment for their employees.

Weaknesses

While the shadow hunter role brings many strengths to an organisation, it's important to be aware of potential weaknesses or challenges that may arise. Here are some considerations regarding the weaknesses of this role:

Introducing a shadow hunter role can be met with **resistance** from individuals or groups within the organisation who may feel threatened or uncomfortable with the examination of hidden aspects of the culture. Overcoming resistance to change and gaining buy-in from all stakeholders can be a potential challenge.

Allocating resources such as time, budget, and personnel to support the shadow hunter role can be a constraint for some organisations. Conducting interviews, organising focus groups, and gathering data require dedicated time and effort. Adequate resources must be allocated to ensure the effectiveness and impact of the shadow hunter's work.

Shadow hunters may come across **sensitive or confidential** information during their investigations. Safeguarding this information and maintaining confidentiality can be a challenge. Establishing clear protocols and ethical guidelines for handling confidential data is essential to address this concern.

The insights and findings of shadow hunters may be subject to **misinterpretation** or miscommunication. It is crucial to effectively communicate the purpose and value of the shadow hunter role to avoid any misunderstandings or misconceptions about their intentions and objectives.

Defining the scope and boundaries of the shadow hunter role is important to prevent potential overlap or conflicts with other roles within the organisation. Clearly delineating responsibilities and establishing effective collaboration channels with other departments or functions is essential to ensure a cohesive and coordinated approach.

Sustaining the impact of the shadow hunter role over the long term can be a challenge. As organisational dynamics evolve, ongoing efforts are required to ensure that the role remains relevant and effective in addressing emerging cultural issues.

Some organisational cultures may be **deeply entrenched** or resistant to change, making it challenging for shadow hunters to bring about meaningful transformation.

Overcoming cultural resistance and building a culture that embraces transparency, inclusivity, and continuous improvement may require substantial time and effort.

Opportunities

The shadow hunter role presents several opportunities for an organisation. Below are some potential opportunities the role brings:

The presence of shadow hunters provides an opportunity to **enhance the overall organisational culture** by uncovering hidden aspects, addressing toxic elements, and fostering transparency. By actively working towards aligning the formal and informal elements of the culture, organisations can create a healthier and more inclusive work environment.

Shadow hunters can play a crucial role in **promoting employee engagement** by actively seeking feedback, addressing concerns, and involving employees in the process of cultural transformation. This involvement fosters a sense of ownership, trust, and empowerment among employees, leading to higher levels of engagement and commitment.

Through their investigations and data gathering activities, shadow hunters can identify the **strengths and weaknesses** of the organisation's culture. This insight allows organisations to capitalise on their strengths and proactively address areas of improvement, thereby enhancing overall performance.

By uncovering hidden aspects of the culture and identifying **potential issues at an early stage,** shadow hunters enable organisations to address these issues proactively. This can prevent conflicts, improve communication, and facilitate prompt resolution of problems, leading to a more harmonious and productive work environment.

Through allowing alignment with strategic goals by identifying cultural elements that may hinder or support the achievement of strategic objectives, organisations can make informed decisions and take targeted actions to ensure **cultural alignment** and facilitate successful strategy execution.

By addressing barriers and fostering a more inclusive and open culture, shadow hunters create an environment conducive to **innovation and creativity**. Employees feel more comfortable expressing their ideas, taking calculated risks, and collaborating across teams, leading to a greater flow of innovative solutions and improved business outcomes.

The presence of shadow hunters encourages a culture of **continuous improvement and learning**. Through their activities, organisations can gather valuable insights, learn from past experiences, and implement targeted interventions to continuously enhance the culture, adapt to changing dynamics, and stay ahead in a competitive landscape.

Organisations that actively promote transparency, inclusivity, and a healthy work environment through the presence of shadow hunters can **enhance their employer brand**. This can attract top talent, improve employee retention, and positively impact the organisation's reputation in the industry.

By leveraging these opportunities, organisations can leverage the shadow hunter role to drive cultural transformation, improve employee experiences, and achieve long-term success.

Threats

While the shadow hunter role offers numerous benefits, it's essential to be aware of potential threats or challenges that may arise. Here are some that could occur:

In some cases, the presence of a shadow hunter role may **trigger political dynamics** within the organisation. Individuals or groups with vested interests in maintaining the current culture may engage in power struggles or attempt to undermine the efforts of shadow hunters. Effective stakeholder management, transparency, and support from leadership are crucial to navigating these political challenges.

While shadow hunters play a valuable role, there is a risk of **overreliance** on their efforts alone. Organisations should avoid viewing the shadow hunter role as a panacea for all cultural challenges and instead foster a culture of shared responsibility for cultural improvement. Collaboration and involvement from leaders, employees, and other stakeholders are essential for sustainable cultural transformation.

Shadow hunters may face challenges in implementing their recommendations or driving change if they **lack the necessary influence** and authority within the organisation. To address this threat, organisations should ensure that shadow hunters have the necessary support, backing from leadership, and access to decision-making processes to effect meaningful change.

The nature of the shadow hunter role involves gathering **sensitive information** about the organisation's culture, including potentially confidential or personal data. Protecting privacy and maintaining confidentiality is paramount. Organisations must establish clear guidelines, policies, and procedures to ensure the ethical and responsible handling of data collected by shadow hunters.

Engaging with the shadow culture and addressing hidden aspects of the organisation can be **emotionally challenging** for shadow hunters. They may encounter negative feedback, or uncover issues that require delicate handling. Providing appropriate support, resources, and mechanisms for self-care and emotional well-being is crucial to mitigate the potential impact on shadow hunters' mental health.

By acknowledging these threats and proactively addressing them, organisations can navigate potential challenges and maximise the positive impact of the shadow hunter role in driving cultural transformation.

The key takeaways in this chapter include:

» Shadow hunters are individuals or groups that play a vital role in unravelling the intricacies of the shadow culture within organisations. They identify and address informal practices, implicit attitudes, and unspoken rules that coexist alongside the official culture.

» They engage in various activities to shed light on the shadow culture. These activities include conducting interviews, facilitating focus groups, observing interactions, and gathering relevant data.

» Shadow hunters collaborate with leaders, employees, and stakeholders to raise awareness, address toxic elements, dismantle silos, and cultivate a healthier and more inclusive work environment. They work together to align the formal and informal aspects of the organisational culture.

» The purpose of the shadow hunter role is to identify and address the hidden aspects of the organisational culture, fostering positive change, transparency, and alignment between formal and informal elements.

» The responsibilities of shadow hunters include actively seeking out hidden elements of the shadow culture, analysing the underlying mechanisms and impact of the shadow culture, gathering relevant data, collaborating with stakeholders, advocating for positive change, and reporting findings and recommendations.

- Organisations need to provide the necessary support and resources to enable shadow hunters to fulfil their responsibilities effectively. This includes access to relevant information, training, and tools. Shadow hunters can also collaborate and share best practices with other shadow hunters within the organisation.

- Shadow hunters actively collaborate with leaders and stakeholders to address the hidden aspects of the shadow culture. They establish relationships, seek input, communicate findings, raise awareness, and work together to eliminate toxic elements, break down silos, and foster inclusivity and respect.

- They play a pivotal role in exposing and transforming the hidden aspects of the organisational culture. They contribute to the enhancement of the overall organisational climate and the experiences of its employees. By promoting transparency, alignment, and positive change, they foster a work environment that promotes health and inclusivity.

CHAPTER 8: Step One – Collaborative Commitment

Chapter pathway

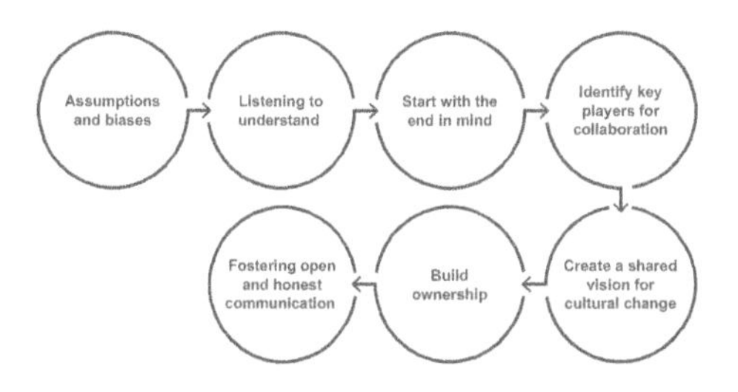

This flowchart gives you a visual outline of the chapter's key points.

Collaborative commitment is a collective dedication and shared responsibility towards a common goal, fostering active participation and mutual support. It plays a pivotal role in any cultural change initiative.

Before embarking on cultural change, it is essential to take stock and understand the potential cultural challenges facing your organisation. By taking time to examine and understand different perceptions, you can ensure your cultural change initiatives are based on a solid foundation of accurate information and insights.

Therefore, this chapter starts at Step One, by discussing the importance of understanding assumptions and biases that may influence decision-making. I will also talk about the importance of listening to understand and how clarifying understanding is a critical communication skill that fosters empathy, improves communication, and prevents misunderstandings. This chapter will also stress the importance of starting a change project with the end in mind to achieve success.

Assumptions and biases

Assumptions and biases can lead us to make inaccurate judgements and decisions, as they are often based on incomplete or biased information, rather than a comprehensive and objective understanding of the situation.

Having an awareness and understanding of different types of bias is a critical first step if you want your change initiative to be a success. There are several types of biases that can exist in companies that we need to be aware of when starting to change the culture. Some of the most common include:

Confirmation bias

This is the tendency to seek out and interpret information in a way that confirms pre-existing beliefs or assumptions. In an organisation setting, this can lead to managers and employees disregarding evidence that contradicts their beliefs or decisions, which can result in poor decision-making.

Availability bias

Availability bias happens when people rely on information that is easily available or memorable, rather than seeking out all relevant information. In an organisation setting, this can result in managers and employees making decisions based on incomplete or biased information, which can lead to poor outcomes.

Unconscious bias

This bias refers to attitudes, beliefs, or stereotypes that we hold at a subconscious level, and that can influence our judgements and behaviours without us being aware of them. These biases can be based on factors such as race, gender, age, or other characteristics, and can lead to unintentional discrimination or unfair treatment of individuals or groups.

Halo effect

When someone makes broad judgements about a person or entity based on a single trait or characteristic, the halo effect occurs. In an organisation setting, this can lead to managers and employees overvaluing certain employees or teams based on a single positive attribute, while undervaluing others who may have different strengths.

Groupthink

Groupthink is the tendency for a group of people to conform to a shared set of beliefs or decisions, even if those decisions are flawed or irrational. In an organisation setting, this can lead to managers and employees making decisions that are not based on evidence or data, but rather on a desire to conform to the group.

Anchoring bias

It's important to not rely too heavily on the first piece of information that is presented when making a decision because when this happens, an anchoring bias is evident. In an organisation setting, this can lead to managers and employees making decisions that are overly influenced by initial data or assumptions, even if those assumptions are flawed.

Overall, biases can have a significant impact on decision-making in companies, and it is essential to be aware of them and take steps to mitigate their effects. This can include seeking out diverse perspectives, gathering and analysing all relevant data, and challenging assumptions and beliefs to ensure that decisions are based on evidence and reason.

Listening to understand

So how can you overcome biases? One way is by listening actively in order to understand someone's perspective, feelings, and needs. By doing this, you are making a deliberate effort to put aside your own assumptions and distractions in order to truly hear and empathise with the other person.

This approach helps you to build stronger relationships with others, foster empathy, and improve communication. It can also help to prevent misunderstandings, reduce conflict, and promote effective problem-solving.

Listening to understand requires a combination of attentive listening, questioning, and reflection. It involves paying close attention to the speaker's words, tone of voice, body language, and context to gain a deeper understanding of their message. It also requires asking open-ended questions to clarify any points of confusion and reflecting back on what you have heard to ensure you are interpreting the message correctly.

Clarifying understanding of what has been said and agreed is a critical component of effective communication. When people communicate, there is always a risk of misunderstanding, misinterpreting, or misremembering what was said. Therefore, it is essential to clarify and confirm that both parties have the same understanding of what has been said and agreed upon. This helps to prevent confusion, conflict, and mistakes. Clarification can involve summarising the key points of the conversation, asking questions to clarify any points of confusion, and reflecting back on what you have heard to ensure that you have interpreted the message correctly.

By way of an example, I once attended a leadership development course at which one of the sessions was all about the importance of clarification. We were all invited to sit in a circle and clarify what we meant when we used the word "confidential". I was confident that I knew what it meant and that it would not take much time to agree on its meaning; however, the other people in that circle had slightly different views than mine. After debating this all morning we agreed that the meaning of the word confidential can vary depending on the context, the specific obligations, and expectations associated with it in each situation. This exercise was a valuable lesson for me in the importance of clarifying exactly what we mean, hear, and understand.

Clarifying understanding is especially important when it comes to agreements or commitments. If you have agreed to something with another person, it is essential to clarify the details and ensure that everyone understands what is expected of them, preventing misunderstandings and helping to build trust.

Start with the end in mind

Starting a change project with the end in mind is a critical step towards achieving collaborative commitment. When you begin a project, I am sure you will agree that it is easy to get caught up in the details and lose sight of the big picture. I have often found myself distracted by a key finding and ended up down a rabbit hole. However, if you start by defining the end goal and working backwards, you can ensure that every step you take is aligned with your ultimate objective.

This approach enables you to identify the key milestones, tasks, and resources required to achieve your goal and helps you to avoid getting sidetracked and ending up down a rabbit hole. By starting with the end in mind, you can also gain a clearer understanding of what success looks like and can measure progress towards your goal.

This clarity of purpose and focus can help you stay motivated and engaged throughout the project and can increase the likelihood of achieving your desired outcomes. Ultimately, starting with the end in mind can set a strong foundation for success and ensures that your efforts are focused on achieving your goal. It helps you stay in your lane on the motorway, so to speak, instead of visiting all the small villages on the way to your destination.

A few examples to help you "start with the end in mind" could be to use one or more of the following:

- Create a vision board for what success looks like in, say, five years' time
- Create and agree on success criteria

- Identify Key Performance Indicators (KPIs) such as:
  - establishing baseline measures
  - determining success benchmarks
  - aligning success metrics with organisational goals
  - developing success tracking systems
  - measuring progress towards success
  - identifying areas for improvement.

And please, don't underestimate the hugely important, and often overlooked, element of any great engaging journey is celebrating successes along the way, remembering the famous quote by Ralph Waldo Emerson: "It's not the destination, it's the journey."

Identify key players for collaboration

Getting the right people in the room is essential for creating your shared vision for cultural change. Building ownership, buy-in and commitment to the change from the start will be key to the success of the transformation. So, identifying key internal and external stakeholders is a vital first step in this process.

To clarify, when I talk about **internal** stakeholders, I am referring to individuals or groups within your organisation who have an interest in or are affected by the cultural change process. They can include executives, managers, frontline employees, and even employee representatives such as unions or employee councils. Identifying internal stakeholders is important because they will be directly involved in the change journey, and their support is essential for success.

When I talk about **external** stakeholders in this context, I refer to individuals or groups outside your organisation who have an interest in or are affected by the cultural change process. They can include customers, suppliers, partners, regulators, and other stakeholders in your industry or community. Identifying external stakeholders is important because they can provide valuable feedback and support for the change journey, and their involvement can help ensure the change effort aligns with the needs and expectations of the broader community. They can also help challenge any bias that we talked about earlier in the chapter as they will often have a very different view of the organisation's culture than employees working within the organisation.

To identify stakeholders, you can use tools such as stakeholder mapping (where you identify your key stakeholders and their needs), customer feedback, or an organisational chart. Once you have identified stakeholders, it is essential to assess their influence and interest in the change effort. This assessment can help you determine which stakeholders to engage more deeply and how to tailor your engagement approach.

Create a shared vision for cultural change

A shared vision for cultural change is critical for building ownership and commitment to the process, so that you can define a common purpose that aligns with your organisation's values and goals.

Your organisation's purpose statement should define why you exist, what you stand for, and what you hope to achieve through your cultural change efforts. It should be clear, concise, and easily understood by all stakeholders. A well-crafted purpose statement can help rally employees around a common goal and align cultural change efforts with the organisation's strategy.

To define your organisation's purpose, you can start by reviewing your existing mission, vision, and values statements. These statements can provide a foundation for defining your purpose and help ensure alignment with your organisation's core beliefs and objectives.

Once the purpose statement is defined, it is essential to communicate it effectively to all stakeholders. This communication should be tailored to different stakeholder groups and use a range of communication channels, including social media, email, and face-to-face conversations.

To monitor progress towards the shared purpose, you can regularly review the aforementioned KPIs and regularly evaluate progress towards the purpose. This evaluation can help identify areas for improvement and ensure the purpose statement remains relevant and aligned with the organisation's evolving needs.

Build ownership

In project management, there are two important roles that define the responsibilities and authority of project team members: the responsible person and the accountable person. These roles are critical to ensure that project tasks are completed on time, within budget, and to the desired quality standards.

The **responsible** person is the team member who is responsible for completing a particular task or activity. They are the ones who perform the work and are expected to ensure that the task is completed on time and to the required standards. The responsible person must have the necessary skills and resources to complete the task, and they must communicate progress to the accountable person.

The **accountable** person is the team member who is ultimately responsible for the success or failure of the project. They are the ones who make the final decision and have the authority to delegate tasks to the responsible person. The accountable person ensures that the project stays on track and that all team members are working towards the same goal. They are also responsible for communicating the project's progress to stakeholders and ensuring that the project is completed within the allocated budget.

Both roles are crucial to the success of a project. The responsible person ensures that individual tasks are completed efficiently and effectively, while the accountable person ensures that the project as a whole is progressing towards the desired outcome. Without a clear understanding of who is responsible and who is accountable for each task, it can be difficult to manage project risks and deliverables effectively.

Effective communication is also essential for the success of both roles. The responsible person must communicate progress and any issues they encounter to the accountable person in a timely and transparent manner. The accountable person must also communicate updates to stakeholders, including progress, delays, and changes to the project scope.

Fostering open and honest communication

The last point to cover in this chapter is the importance of candour, meaning the quality of being honest, open, and transparent in communication, especially in difficult or sensitive situations. In the context of a culture change project, candour is essential for creating a culture of trust and accountability, which is critical for achieving successful outcomes.

Cultural change projects often involve making significant changes to the way things are done, which can be challenging and uncomfortable for some individuals or groups. Open and honest communication can help to address any concerns, fears, or resistance that may arise during the change process. By acknowledging and addressing these issues, stakeholders can work together to find solutions and move towards the desired outcome.

Candour also promotes accountability, which is crucial for ensuring that individuals and organisations are responsible for their actions and decisions; this can help to identify areas where improvements are needed and to hold individuals and organisations accountable for making changes.

Your call to action

By embracing collaborative commitment, you can become a catalyst for positive transformation. My invitation to you now is to foster collaborative commitment and drive cultural change in your organisation by reflecting on your biases and assumptions, actively listening, envisioning the end goal, involving key players in the change, creating a shared vision, and encouraging open communication. Not only will you create a more inclusive and engaging work environment, but you will also start to unlock the full potential of your colleagues and pave the way for sustainable success.

Embracing collaborative commitment allows you to be at the forefront of positive transformation, shaping the culture of your organisation for the better.

Take action now and make a lasting impact!

The key takeaways in this chapter include:

- Before initiating a cultural change initiative, it is crucial to take stock of the perceived cultural challenges facing the organisation.
- Assumptions and biases can lead to inaccurate judgements and decisions and need to be addressed. Different types of biases can exist in companies, including confirmation bias, availability bias, unconscious bias, halo effect, groupthink, and anchoring bias. It is important to be aware of biases and take steps to mitigate their effects.
- Listening to understand is a crucial communication skill that involves actively listening to someone in order to comprehend their perspective, feelings, and needs.
- Starting a change project with the end in mind is a critical step towards achieving success. It helps you to stay focused on the project goals and not get lost in the details.
- Engaging and involving employees at all levels of the organisation increases ownership and commitment to the change journey, leading to better outcomes and sustained cultural transformation.
- Clear, transparent, and consistent communication helps align employees with the vision, goals, and progress of the change initiative so that it becomes a shared vision. It fosters understanding, reduces resistance, and builds trust, enabling smoother cultural transitions.

- By fostering an inclusive environment and actively addressing biases, organisations can create a culture that values diversity and promotes fairness and equal opportunity, all within the context of building ownership.

- Clarifying understanding through fostering open communication is a critical component of effective communication to ensure that both parties have the same understanding of what has been said and agreed.

CHAPTER 9: Step Two – Cultural Compass

Chapter pathway

Before you can begin to identify areas for improvement or develop a plan for cultural change, you need to have a clear understanding of your current culture, which is Step Two of the Cultural Change Programme. There are various ways you can do this. One approach is to conduct a cultural audit, which involves a detailed assessment of your organisation's values, beliefs, practices, and norms. This can be done through surveys, interviews, focus groups, or other methods of data collection. You may also want to analyse your organisation's history, mission statement, policies and procedures, and any other relevant documents to gain insights into the underlying values and beliefs that drive your culture.

Another approach is to observe the behaviours and interactions of employees, customers, and other stakeholders. This can help you identify patterns and behaviours that may be contributing to or detracting from your organisation's culture. For example, if your organisation values collaboration and teamwork, but you notice that employees are frequently working in silos or competing with each other, this may indicate a disconnect between your culture and your actual practices.

Understanding your organisation culture is a critical first step in driving cultural change. It provides the foundation for identifying areas for improvement and developing effective strategies for creating a culture that drives success and fosters employee satisfaction. Let's start this chapter by looking at why you should measure your organisation culture.

Measuring your organisation culture

One question I am often asked by managers and HR professionals is should I measure the current culture? Although carrying out a cultural audit is common practice, I believe the answer should depend upon the context and the goals of the organisation as well as the methodology that might be used.

Assessing organisation culture through a cultural audit is particularly important for high-performing companies that aim to maintain their success by fostering a positive work environment. It can provide insights into the organisation's values, beliefs, and behaviours, which are essential components of a successful work culture. By identifying areas where cultural changes may be needed, high-performing companies can ensure that they are creating an inclusive environment that values and respects all employees.

However, there can be potential drawbacks to measuring culture. Attempts to measure culture may oversimplify or misrepresent it, as organisation culture is a multifaceted concept that is difficult to measure comprehensively. Furthermore, the methods used to measure culture may be biased and reflect the perspectives of the individuals or groups who developed them. Measuring culture can also stigmatise certain groups or individuals who do not fit within the dominant culture, and raise privacy concerns and ethical issues, as it may involve collecting personal information. Therefore, careful consideration of the potential benefits and drawbacks of measuring organisation culture is necessary first.

In the article, "Measuring culture – can it be done?" the authors suggest: "While there are challenges with measuring cultures, such as social desirability, subjectivity, and sampling errors, advances in organisational psychology, computing power, and technology may enable unobtrusive culture measurement without ever entering an organisation."[9] Overall, the article suggests that culture can be measured and managed, and it is essential to do so for organisations to be successful in an increasingly complex and uncertain world.

Another article states that: "A business's culture can catalyse or undermine success. Yet the tools available for measuring it – namely, employee surveys and questionnaires – have significant shortcomings. Employee self-reports are often unreliable. The values and beliefs that people say are important to them, for example, are often not reflected in how they actually behave. Moreover, surveys provide static, or at best episodic, snapshots of organisations that are constantly evolving."[10]

Ultimately, measuring and managing culture is essential for organisations to be successful in an increasingly complex and uncertain world, but careful consideration of the potential benefits and drawbacks is necessary before conducting a cultural audit.

When looking at the insights from my survey mentioned in the introductory chapter to this book, organisation leaders told me they used various tools and methods to monitor and change their current cultures, with varying degrees of success.

They employed a diverse range of tools and methods to monitor and transform their existing cultures, each yielding varying degrees of success. These approaches encompassed regular pulse surveys, staff surveys, and focus groups to assess employee opinions and perceptions. Additionally, they organised a mix of social and work-based events, led by both management and staff, to reinforce organisational values and promote cohesion. Objective setting and regular updates, quality conversations, recruitment practices, and networking with partner organisations were also instrumental in shaping the work environment.

Moreover, the organisation invested in maintaining a positive work environment through various means, such as providing comfortable furnishings and implementing awards and rewards structures. They also hosted guest speaker sessions covering essential topics like equality, diversity, inclusion, well-being, and mental health. Furthermore, feedback-driven methods played a crucial role in evaluating the culture, including employee surveys, breakout groups, exit interviews, and appraisals. The use of tools like Culture Amp, internal and external surveys, employee voice, values, charters, and well-being assessments provided valuable insights.

Finally, some of the organisations engaged in meaningful discussions with managers facilitated working groups, and participated in programmes like Best Companies, Investors in Diversity, and Join the Conversation to gain further understanding and perspectives on their organisational culture.

Let's now look at the positives and negatives of the following methods of measuring the culture in more detail: cultural surveys, interviews, focus groups, direct observation, performance metrics, cultural artefacts, employee feedback mechanisms, the power of visuals, and haiku poetry.

Cultural surveys

One of the most popular ways companies try to collect cultural information is via a survey of some kind. It typically involves collecting data from employees through a questionnaire or survey that asks them about their perceptions of the organisation's culture, values, beliefs, attitudes, and behaviours. Surveys can be designed to measure specific aspects of culture, such as diversity and inclusion, leadership effectiveness, employee engagement, or overall organisational culture. For some examples of survey questions that you can download, please visit https://hrfusion.podia.com/shadow-cultures-bonuses or use the QR code.

The data collected from these surveys can be used to identify areas of strength and weakness in the organisation culture and to inform decisions about changes or improvements that can be made to create a more positive and effective work environment. Cultural surveys can also be used to track changes in the organisation culture over time and to evaluate the effectiveness of initiatives aimed at improving the culture.

Positives of using surveys:

- Surveys can help individuals or organisations gain a deeper understanding of the cultural norms, values, and practices of a particular group of people. This can help to build bridges across cultural divides and promote mutual understanding.
- They can identify areas for improvement where there are gaps between an organisation's cultural values and its actual practices. This can help to highlight areas for improvement and inform cultural change initiatives.
- By gaining a deeper understanding of cultural differences, individuals and organisations can avoid unintentional cultural misunderstandings that could harm relationships and hinder collaboration.
- Cultural surveys can provide a basis for benchmarking an organisation's cultural performance against industry standards or best practices. This can help to identify areas of strength and weakness and inform strategies for improvement.

Negatives of using surveys:

- Surveys may oversimplify complex cultural dynamics by reducing them to a set of standardised questions or metrics. This can lead to a superficial understanding of cultural norms and practices.
- They may not capture the full range of cultural experiences and perspectives within a particular group

of people. This can lead to a lack of nuance in the results and a failure to account for individual differences.

- As surveys rely on self-reported data, they may be subject to response bias. Participants may be hesitant to report negative experiences or may respond in a way that they believe is socially desirable.
- The design of a cultural survey may not be culturally appropriate for all groups of people. Questions that are relevant in one culture may not be relevant or appropriate in another, leading to inaccurate or incomplete results.

Surveys are a popular way for companies to assess and measure the culture within an organisation. They can identify areas of strength and weakness, track changes over time, and evaluate the effectiveness of cultural change initiatives. However, they may oversimplify complex cultural dynamics, not capture the full range of experiences and perspectives, be subject to response bias, and not be culturally appropriate for all groups of people.

Interviews

Interviews can be used to gather qualitative data on employee experiences and perceptions of organisation culture. They can provide more in-depth insights than surveys and allow for follow-up questions and clarification. By conducting interviews, you can gather first-hand information about the experiences, perceptions, and values of individuals within the organisation.

Interviews can be conducted in a structured or unstructured format, depending on the goals of the assessment. Structured interviews involve a predetermined set of questions, which allows for a consistent approach to data collection and facilitates comparisons between participants. Unstructured interviews, on the other hand, are more open-ended and allow for a more in-depth exploration of individual experiences and perspectives.

When conducting interviews to assess organisation culture, it is important to ensure that the process is confidential and anonymous. This helps to create a safe and trusting environment where individuals feel comfortable sharing their honest opinions and experiences.

Interviews can provide a wealth of information about an organisation's culture, including its values, communication style, leadership approach, and employee satisfaction. This information can be used to identify areas for improvement, inform cultural change initiatives, and monitor progress over time.

Positives of using interviews:

- Interviews allow for in-depth exploration of individual experiences and perspectives, which can provide a more nuanced understanding of an organisation's culture than surveys or other methods of data collection.
- They provide rich, qualitative data that is difficult to capture through quantitative measures. This type of data can help to highlight underlying issues and provide insights into the root causes of cultural dynamics within an organisation.
- When conducted appropriately, interviews can create a safe and confidential environment where individuals feel comfortable sharing their honest opinions and experiences. This can help to ensure that the data collected is accurate and representative of the experiences of employees and other stakeholders.
- Interviews allow for follow-up questions and probing, which can help to clarify responses and gather more detailed information.

Negatives of using interviews:

- Conducting interviews can be time-consuming, especially if a large number of participants are involved. This can be a significant investment of time and resources for organisations.
- They may be subject to interviewer bias, which can occur when the interviewer's personal opinions or beliefs influence the questions asked or the interpretation of the responses.
- Interviews may not be representative of the experiences and perspectives of all employees or stakeholders within an organisation. People who are willing to participate in interviews may not be representative of the broader population.
- Participants may be influenced by social desirability bias, which can occur when individuals provide responses that they believe are socially acceptable, rather than their true opinions or experiences.

Interviews can be an effective method for assessing organisation culture, but it is important to carefully consider the potential benefits and drawbacks before deciding to use this method. Conducting interviews in a thoughtful and systematic manner can help to mitigate some of the potential drawbacks and ensure that the data collected is accurate and useful.

Focus groups

Focus groups involve a small group of employees discussing their experiences and perceptions of organisational culture in a facilitated group discussion. They can provide valuable insights into group dynamics and interactions within the organisation.

They can be used to explore a wide range of topics related to organisation cultures, such as communication styles, leadership approaches, employee satisfaction, and work-life balance. The discussions that take place during focus groups can provide valuable qualitative data that is difficult to capture through other methods of data collection.

When conducting focus groups to assess organisation culture, it is important to ensure that the process is confidential and anonymous. This helps to create a safe and trusting environment where participants feel comfortable sharing their honest opinions and experiences.

Focus groups can be conducted in person or online, depending on the needs of the organisation and the preferences of the participants. They can be moderated by a trained facilitator who guides the discussion and ensures that all participants have an opportunity to share their views.

The knowledge acquired from focus groups can be harnessed to pinpoint areas that require improvement, guide cultural change endeavours, and track progress over time.

Focus groups can also help to build a sense of community and engagement among employees by providing a platform for open and honest communication.

Positives of using focus groups:

- Focus groups allow for interactive and dynamic discussion among participants, which can lead to the emergence of new insights and ideas that may not have been uncovered through individual interviews or surveys.
- Like interviews, focus groups can provide rich, qualitative data that is difficult to capture through quantitative measures. This type of data can help to identify

underlying issues and provide insights into the root causes of cultural dynamics within an organisation.

- By providing a platform for open and honest communication, focus groups can help to build a sense of community and engagement among employees. This can improve morale and foster a positive organisational culture.
- They provide a forum to gain the views of a range of different stakeholders within an organisation, such as employees, managers, and executives. This can help to ensure that the data collected is representative of the experiences of a diverse range of individuals.

Negatives of using focus groups:

- Focus groups may be subject to groupthink, which can occur when participants conform to the opinions of the group rather than express their own views.
- They can be influenced by dominant voices, which can occur when one or a few individuals dominate the conversation and prevent others from sharing their opinions.
- Participants in focus groups may be influenced by social desirability bias, which can occur when individuals provide responses that they believe are socially acceptable, rather than their true opinions or experiences.
- Like interviews, focus groups can be time-consuming, especially if a large number of participants are involved. This can be a significant investment of time and resources for organisations.

Focus groups can be an effective method for assessing organisation culture, but it is important to carefully consider the potential benefits and drawbacks before deciding to use this method. Conducting focus groups in a thoughtful and systematic manner can help to mitigate some of the potential drawbacks and ensure that the data collected is accurate and useful.

Direct observation

Observation involves studying employee behaviours and interactions in the workplace. It can provide insights into how the organisation's culture is manifested in daily work practices.

The observations can be structured, with predefined criteria for what to observe, or unstructured, allowing for the observer to capture what they find important. The data collected through observations can be analysed qualitatively or quantitatively, depending on the research question and goals of the assessment. Overall, observations can provide a rich and nuanced understanding of organisation culture, but it is important to ensure that the observations are conducted in an ethical and respectful manner, with the appropriate consent and involvement of employees.

Positives of using direct observation:

- Observations can provide direct, first-hand insights into how employees behave and interact with each other, which can help to identify cultural norms, values, and beliefs.
- They can capture non-verbal cues, such as body language and tone of voice, that may not be captured through other methods, such as surveys or interviews.
- Direct observations provide a holistic view of organisation culture, as they can cover a wide range of activities, work areas, and interactions within the organisation.
- They can provide insights for specific improvements, such as communication, collaboration, or leadership.

Negatives of using direct observation:

- Observations can be time-consuming, especially if they are conducted over an extended period or across multiple locations within the organisation.
- Observations can be influenced by observer bias, which can occur when the observer's expectations or assumptions influence their interpretation of what they see. This can lead to inaccurate or incomplete data.
- Observations can only capture observable behaviours, and they may not be able to provide insights into employees' thoughts, feelings, or motivations.
- There are ethical considerations, as they involve directly observing employees without their knowledge or consent. It is important to ensure that ethical guidelines are followed and that employees are informed about the observations and given the opportunity to opt out if they wish.

Observations can be a valuable method for assessing organisational culture, but they should be used in combination with other methods, such as surveys or interviews, to ensure that a comprehensive view of organisational culture is obtained. It is important to carefully consider the positives and negatives of observations and to plan them carefully to ensure that they are conducted in an ethical and respectful manner.

Performance metrics

Performance metrics, such as employee turnover rates, productivity, and customer satisfaction, can provide indirect indicators of organisation culture. High turnover rates or low productivity may indicate issues with the current culture.

By analysing performance metrics, organisations can gain valuable insights into how cultural factors impact business outcomes and identify areas where cultural improvements can be made.

These metrics can be collected through various sources, such as employee surveys, HR records, financial reports, or customer feedback. The data can be analysed using statistical methods to identify patterns, trends, or correlations between cultural factors and business outcomes. The analysis can also be used to benchmark the organisation's performance against industry standards or competitors.

They can also provide a data-driven approach to assessing organisational culture, which can be useful for decision-making and resource allocation. However, it is important to ensure that the metrics chosen are relevant, valid, and reliable and that they are not used in isolation from other methods, such as surveys or interviews. It is also important to recognise that performance metrics only provide indirect insights into organisational culture and may not capture the full complexity of cultural factors.

Positives of using performance metrics:

- Performance metrics provide objective and measurable data, which can be useful for identifying trends, patterns, and areas for improvement.
- They are easy to compare over time or against industry standards or competitors, which can provide valuable insights into the organisation's performance and cultural strengths and weaknesses.
- They reflect the impact of culture, such as employee engagement, communication, or leadership, on business outcomes, such as productivity, customer satisfaction, or profitability.

- Performance metrics can inform decision-making and resource allocation, such as identifying areas where cultural improvements can lead to better business outcomes.

Negatives of using performance metrics:

- Performance metrics only provide indirect insights into organisation culture, and they may not capture the full complexity of cultural factors or the experiences and perspectives of employees.
- They can be influenced by external factors, such as economic conditions, market trends, or industry changes, which can make it difficult to isolate the impact of cultural factors on business outcomes.
- They may incentivise short-term thinking or prioritise quantitative outcomes over qualitative aspects of organisation culture, such as employee well-being or ethical practices.
- This may create unintended consequences, such as employees focusing solely on meeting performance targets, which may lead to neglecting other important aspects of their work or culture.

Performance metrics, including turnover, productivity, and customer satisfaction, can offer insights into organisational culture. However, their relevance, validity, and limitations must be considered, and multiple data sources should be used to assess the cultural impact on outcomes.

Cultural artefacts

Cultural artefacts refer to tangible objects, symbols, or practices that represent the values, beliefs, and traditions of a culture.

In the context of assessing organisation culture, cultural artefacts can include physical objects, such as office layout, decor, or workwear, as well as more intangible aspects, such as language, rituals, or norms. By analysing cultural artefacts, organisations can gain insights into the underlying values and assumptions that shape their culture, as well as identify areas where cultural improvements can be made.

Cultural artefacts can be collected through various methods, such as observation, interviews, or surveys. They can be analysed using qualitative methods, such as content analysis or discourse analysis, to identify themes or patterns that reflect the organisation's culture. Cultural artefacts can also be compared to other organisations or cultural norms to identify differences or similarities in cultural values and practices.

Positives of using cultural artefacts:

- Cultural artefacts provide tangible evidence of the organisation's culture, which can help to identify patterns, values, and beliefs that shape organisational behaviour.
- They can provide unique insights into the organisation's culture that may not be captured by other methods, such as surveys or interviews.
- Cultural artefacts can be compared across organisations or cultures to identify similarities or differences in values and practices.
- Analysing cultural artefacts can identify areas where cultural improvements can be made, which can inform efforts to change organisational culture.

Negatives of using cultural artefacts:

- Cultural artefacts may not represent the full complexity of the organisational culture and may be subject to interpretation or bias.

- Analysing cultural artefacts can be difficult, as different individuals may interpret them differently.
- They may be influenced by external factors, such as industry norms or societal trends, which can make it difficult to isolate the impact of organisational culture.
- They may not capture employee perspectives or experiences, who may have different interpretations or experiences of organisational culture.

Cultural artefacts can provide a valuable method for assessing organisational culture, as they can provide tangible evidence of the underlying values and assumptions that shape organisational behaviour. However, it is important to recognise that cultural artefacts may not represent the full complexity of organisational culture, and they may be subject to interpretation or bias.

Employee feedback mechanisms

Employee feedback mechanisms refer to the processes and tools that organisations use to gather feedback from their employees. In the context of assessing organisation culture, employee feedback mechanisms can include surveys, focus groups, one-to-one interviews, suggestion boxes, or online platforms that allow employees to provide anonymous feedback.

By gathering feedback from employees, organisations can gain valuable insights into the strengths and weaknesses of their culture, as well as identify areas for improvement. Employee feedback can also help to identify the factors that contribute to employee engagement, motivation, and job satisfaction, which are critical for attracting and retaining top talent.

Employee feedback systems can be designed to gather feedback on specific aspects of organisation culture, such as communication, leadership, or collaboration, or they can be more general in nature, asking employees to provide feedback on their overall experiences at the organisation. Organisations can also use employee feedback mechanisms to track changes in culture over time, by administering surveys or other feedback mechanisms on a regular basis.

Positives of using employee feedback mechanisms:

- Employee feedback mechanisms allow organisations to hear directly from their employees and gain insights into their experiences and perspectives.
- They can help organisations identify areas where they excel, as well as areas where improvements can be made.
- By gathering feedback from employees, organisations can identify factors that contribute to employee engagement, motivation, and job satisfaction, which are critical for attracting and retaining top talent.
- They can track changes over time, by administering surveys or other feedback mechanisms on a regular basis.

Negatives of using employee feedback mechanisms:

- They may not capture the full complexity of organisational culture and may be subject to interpretation or bias.
- They may not be representative of all employees, particularly if certain groups are less likely to participate.
- Employee feedback may be influenced by external factors, such as the current economic or political climate, which can make it difficult to isolate the impact of organisational culture.

- Organisations must act on the feedback they receive for employee feedback mechanisms to be effective. If employees feel that their feedback is not taken seriously or acted upon, they may become disengaged or cynical.

Employee feedback mechanisms can provide a valuable method for assessing organisational culture, as they allow organisations to hear directly from their employees and gain insights into their experiences and perspectives. However, it is important to design feedback mechanisms carefully to ensure that they are effective, and to act on the feedback that is received to drive meaningful change within the organisation.

Haiku poetry

The above methods for collecting data are much more popular than this one. However, I wanted to add it to demonstrate that you do not have to follow what is popular; you can try something different.

Haiku poetry is a form of Japanese poetry that consists of three lines. The first and third lines have five syllables, while the second line has seven syllables. While haiku poetry is often associated with nature, it can also be used to explore and assess organisational culture.

Using haiku poetry to assess organisational culture involves encouraging employees to write haiku poems that capture their experiences, perceptions, and values related to this. Haiku poetry can provide a unique and creative perspective on an organisation's culture that may be difficult to capture through more traditional methods of data collection.

An example of this poetry is:

Workplace harmony,
Values woven through each thread,
Culture's tapestry.

The above reflects the concept of organisational culture as a harmonious blend of values and behaviours that permeate every aspect of the workplace. It emphasises the idea that culture is not just an abstract concept but a tangible presence that is intricately woven into the fabric of the organisation. The haiku suggests that a strong organisational culture is like a beautiful tapestry, where each thread represents a value or principle that guides the actions and interactions of employees. It highlights the importance of fostering a cohesive and unified culture that influences and shapes the overall atmosphere and dynamics within the workplace.

Haiku poetry could be used to explore a wide range of topics related to organisation cultures, such as communication styles, leadership approaches, employee satisfaction, and work-life balance. The crispness of the form requires careful consideration of word choice, resulting in highly distilled and meaningful expressions.

Haiku poems can be collected anonymously or attributed to the author, depending on the preferences of the organisation and the participants. They can be shared in a variety of formats, such as during meetings or through an internal newsletter, to engage and inspire employees in exploring and reflecting on organisation culture.

The insights gained through haiku poetry can be used to identify areas for improvement, inform cultural change initiatives, and monitor progress over time.

Positives of using haiku poetry:

- Haiku poetry can provide a unique and creative perspective on an organisation culture that may be difficult to capture through more traditional methods of data collection. This can result in insights that may not have been uncovered through other methods.
- Writing haiku poetry encourages employees to reflect on their experiences, perceptions, and values related to the organisation's culture. This can promote self-expression and help to build a sense of community and engagement among employees.
- The brevity of haiku poetry requires careful consideration of word choice and precise communication, resulting in highly distilled and meaningful expressions.
- They can be easily shared and disseminated in a variety of formats, such as during meetings or through an internal newsletter, to engage and inspire employees in exploring and reflecting on organisation culture.

Negatives of using haiku poetry:

- Haiku poetry may not be suitable for all employees. Some may not feel comfortable expressing their thoughts and feelings through this medium.
- While haiku poetry can provide unique and creative insights into organisation culture, it may not provide in-depth insights that can be gained through more structured and extensive methods of data collection, such as surveys or interviews.
- This method may require clarification as it can be open to interpretation, and the meaning of a poem may be unclear or ambiguous. This can make it difficult to draw concrete conclusions from the data collected.
- It may not be appropriate for all organisational cultures, and some cultures may not place a high value on creative expression or reflection.

Using haiku poetry to assess organisation culture can be a creative and unique way to gain insights into an organisation's values, attitudes, and behaviours. However, it is important to carefully consider the potential benefits and drawbacks and to determine whether this method is appropriate for the specific organisation and its employees.

Your call to action

What actions need to happen for your organisation to focus on its cultural compass? Could you implement an audit, behaviour observation, employee perception measurement, or an insightful reflection through poetry? Develop a change strategy, implement it, monitor progress, and adjust strategies based on feedback.

Ultimately, by focusing on your organisation's cultural compass and igniting positive change, you can create an environment where employees thrive and collaboration flourishes. Investing in a strong organisational culture not only benefits your employees but also has a direct impact on your organisation's reputation, performance, and long-term success.

Ignite positive change and create a thriving organisational culture!

The key takeaways in this chapter include:

- There are various ways to measure organisational culture, including surveys, interviews, focus groups, observations, performance metrics, cultural artefacts, and employee feedback mechanisms.
- Each method has its benefits and drawbacks, and it is important to carefully consider which methods are most appropriate for the specific organisation and its employees.
- Surveys are a popular method for measuring culture, but they may oversimplify complex cultural dynamics, not capture the full range of experiences and perspectives, be subject to response bias, and not be culturally appropriate for all groups of people.
- Interviews and focus groups can be effective methods for assessing culture, but they require careful planning and consideration to ensure that the data collected is accurate and useful.
- Observations and performance metrics can indirectly indicate culture, but they should be used in combination with other methods to obtain a comprehensive view of culture.
- Cultural artefacts can provide tangible evidence of underlying values and assumptions, but they may not represent the full complexity of culture and may be subject to interpretation or bias.

- Employee feedback mechanisms, such as pulse surveys, can provide valuable insights into culture, but they require careful design and implementation to be effective.

- Using creative methods, such as haiku poetry, can be a unique way to gain insights into culture, but it is important to carefully consider their benefits and drawbacks before deciding to use them.

CHAPTER 10: Step Three – Continuous Feedback

Chapter pathway

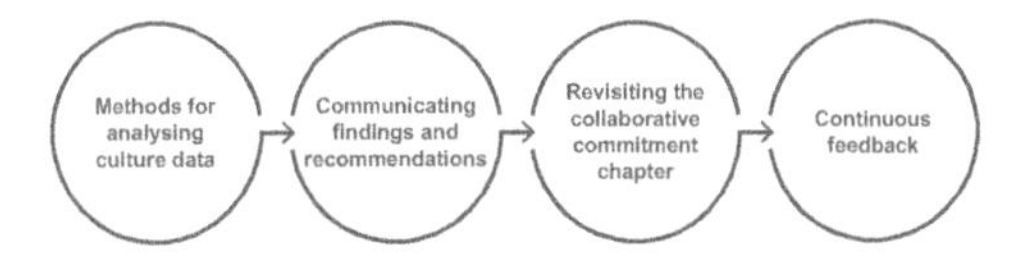

In this chapter, which covers Step Three of the programme, we will look at interpreting the data collected as a crucial step in the research process. After collecting data, the project group must analyse and make sense of their findings to draw meaningful conclusions that can answer their research question or hypothesis. This chapter will provide a detailed examination of the data analysis process, including the techniques used to analyse the data, the results obtained, and the interpretation of those results.

Both interpreting the data collected and feeding back to stakeholders need to be linked, so whilst this chapter is in two parts, I strongly advise that both elements are conducted in parallel to ensure that whilst you are analysing the data collected you are keeping key stakeholders in the loop and informed, helping ensure you keep their engagement in the change journey.

Methods for analysing cultural data

When reviewing data in a change project, several data analysis techniques can be employed, depending on the research questions and the type of data collected. Here are some of the main data analysis techniques that could be used:

Qualitative analysis

Analysing non-numerical data, such as interviews, focus groups, and observations can help identify themes, patterns, and trends in the data and provide rich insights into the attitudes, beliefs, and behaviours of the participants.

Quantitative analysis

Scrutinising numerical data, such as survey responses or performance metrics, can help identify trends and patterns in the data, calculate statistical significance, and test hypotheses.

Content analysis

When you examine the content of written or verbal communication, such as emails, memos, or meeting transcripts, it can help identify themes and patterns in the data, such as the frequency of certain topics or the tone of communication.

Social network analysis

Evaluating the relationships between individuals or groups in a social network can help identify key influencers, communication patterns, and social dynamics that may affect change programmes.

Comparative analysis

When you compare data from different sources, such as before-and-after surveys, to identify changes over time, it can help measure the effectiveness of change efforts and identify areas for improvement.

Overall, the choice of data analysis technique will depend on the specific research questions and the type of data collected in the change project. A combination of these techniques may be used to gain a comprehensive understanding of the data and its implications for the change initiative.

Communicating findings and recommendations

When presenting the findings of a change project, it is important to ensure that the results are communicated effectively and in a way that is easily understood by stakeholders, acknowledging any limitations of the findings that may have affected the data analysis. This could include issues with data collection or analysis, sample size, or other factors that may have impacted the results. Some examples of ways to present the findings are:

Written report

A written report is a comprehensive way to present the findings of a change project. The report should be well organised and clearly structured, with a summary of the research questions, methods used, results obtained, and conclusions drawn. It should be written in clear and concise language and may include tables, graphs, or other visual aids to support the findings.

Presentation

A presentation is an effective way to share the key findings. The presentation should also be well organised and visually appealing, with clear and concise slides that summarise the research questions, methods used, and results obtained. It should highlight the main conclusions and recommendations of the project.

Infographics

Infographics are a visually appealing way to present the findings. They can be used to highlight key statistics or trends in the data in a simple and easy-to-understand format. Infographics can be posted on social media or distributed as part of a report or presentation.

Dashboard

A dashboard is an interactive tool that presents the data in a visual format, allowing stakeholders to explore the data in real time. It can be customised to highlight specific metrics or trends and can be accessed by stakeholders through a web portal or mobile application.

Video

A video is an engaging way to present the findings. It can be used to showcase the key findings and highlight the impact of the change initiative on the organisation. The video should be well produced and visually appealing, with clear and concise messaging.

The final choice of presentation method will depend on the audience and the purpose of the communication. The findings should be presented in a way that is easily understood and relevant to the stakeholders' needs.

Revisiting the Collaborative Commitment chapter

It is wise at this stage to revisit Chapter 8 to help ensure you are still working in partnership with your stakeholders, as this is not a one-time commitment but rather an ongoing process that requires a sustained commitment from all parties involved. As a result, it is important to periodically revisit and ensure that all parties are still aligned with the goals, objectives, and expectations of the change programme.

Continuous feedback

Once you have analysed the initial data, the second part of this process is to look at how you can implement continuous feedback as an essential aspect of creating and sustaining a positive and productive organisational culture, especially when undergoing a change programme.

By regularly collecting feedback from employees and project group members, organisations can identify strengths and weaknesses in their change management processes and make informed decisions about necessary changes and improvements to create a successful and positive change journey. Furthermore, regular feedback ensures that employees feel valued and heard, leading to increased engagement and retention.

To assist with this, I have developed the RATICA framework: a set of six key elements of continuous feedback for improving communication whilst undergoing a change journey. RATICA stands for **R**egularity, **A**ctionability, **T**ransparency, **I**nclusivity, **C**ommunication and Engagement, and **A**ccountability. By incorporating these elements into feedback mechanisms, organisations can enhance their change journey and create a more effective and positive work environment.

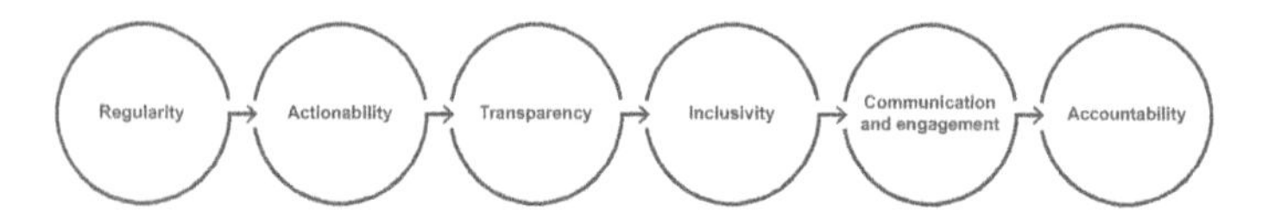

Regularity

The regularity of feedback refers to the frequency and consistency with which feedback is collected from employees within an organisation. It entails establishing a systematic approach to gathering feedback on an ongoing basis rather than relying solely on sporadic or infrequent feedback collection efforts.

When organisations get feedback regularly, it means that they can have a structured and planned approach to collecting information from employees at predetermined intervals or as part of a continuous feedback loop. This allows for a consistent flow of feedback, enabling organisations to track changes, trends, and patterns in employee perceptions, opinions, and experiences over time. It also ensures that feedback is current, relevant, and up to date, providing a comprehensive picture of the workforce's sentiments and enabling companies to make informed decisions and take appropriate actions.

Actionability

The actionability of feedback refers to the extent to which feedback collected from employees can be translated into meaningful and actionable changes or improvements in the organisation. Actionable feedback provides clear and specific insights that can be used to drive positive change or address identified areas of concern.

It goes beyond general feedback or vague suggestions and provides practical recommendations or suggestions that can be implemented to make tangible improvements. Actionable feedback is specific, relevant, and aligned with the goals and objectives of the organisation, allowing for targeted interventions and actions to be taken based on the feedback received. Organisations should prioritise collecting actionable feedback to ensure that it can be effectively utilised to drive positive changes, enhance employee engagement and satisfaction, and improve overall organisational performance.

Transparency

Transparency of feedback refers to the openness and honesty with which feedback is collected, shared, and used within an organisation. It involves creating an environment where feedback is encouraged, valued, and shared in a transparent manner, without fear of reprisal or negative consequences.

Transparent feedback entails providing employees with clear and timely information about the purpose, process, and outcomes of feedback collection efforts, as well as how the feedback will be used by the organisation. This includes sharing feedback results, trends, and actions taken based on the feedback received from employees and relevant stakeholders.

It also involves ensuring that feedback is provided in a constructive and respectful manner, focusing on areas of improvement rather than personal criticism. Transparent feedback practices promote trust, openness, and accountability within the organisation, and foster a culture of continuous improvement and learning. They allow employees to have confidence that their feedback is being taken seriously and used to drive positive change, leading to improved employee engagement and morale.

Inclusivity

Inclusivity of feedback refers to ensuring that feedback collection initiatives within an organisation are inclusive, equitable, and accessible to all employees, regardless of their background, identity, or position. It involves creating a feedback process that recognises and respects diversity and actively seeks feedback from all employees, including those from underrepresented or marginalised groups. Inclusive feedback practices aim to create a safe and supportive environment where all employees feel empowered and encouraged to share their perspectives, opinions, and experiences without fear of bias, discrimination, or exclusion.

Communication and engagement

Effective communication and engagement of feedback are crucial elements in the feedback process within an organisation. Communication of feedback entails conveying feedback to employees in a clear, timely, and constructive manner. It involves utilising appropriate communication channels and techniques to ensure that the feedback is well received and understood by the intended recipients.

By fostering open lines of communication and engaging employees in the feedback process, organisations can enhance employee engagement, facilitate understanding, and promote effective action based on the feedback received. The communication and engagement of feedback play a pivotal role in driving continuous improvement and development within the organisation.

Accountability

Accountability of feedback refers to the responsibility and ownership that individuals and organisations have in taking action based on the feedback received. It involves holding individuals, teams, and the organisation as a whole responsible for using feedback to drive positive change, improve performance, and achieve desired outcomes. Accountability is a critical aspect of the feedback process as it ensures that feedback is not only collected and shared but also acted upon in a meaningful way.

Your call to action

My invitation to you is to consider now the best way you can implement a culture of continuous improvement through regularity, actionability, transparency, inclusivity, communication and engagement, and accountability. What is the first thing you need to do to create a positive organisational culture through the power of continuous feedback? By setting this foundation, you lay the groundwork for ongoing growth, collaboration, and excellence within your organisation.

A culture of continuous improvement will foster innovation, drive performance, and create an environment where individuals and teams thrive. Don't delay – take the first step today and unlock the power of continuous feedback to create a positive and impactful organisational culture.

The key takeaways in this chapter include:

- After collecting data in a culture change project, it is crucial to analyse and make sense of the findings to draw meaningful conclusions. Data analysis techniques such as qualitative analysis, quantitative analysis, content analysis, social network analysis, and comparative analysis can be used depending on the type of data collection and research questions.

- When presenting the findings of a culture change project, it is important to communicate the results effectively and in a way that is easily understood by stakeholders. This can be done through written reports, presentations, infographics, dashboards, or videos, depending on the audience and purpose of the communication.

- It is important to periodically revisit the collaborative commitment chapter (Chapter 8) to ensure that all parties involved in the change programme are still aligned with the goals, objectives, and expectations of the change journey. This helps to maintain a sustained commitment from all stakeholders throughout the change process.

- Continuous feedback is crucial in creating and sustaining a positive and productive organisational culture during a change programme. Regularly collecting feedback from employees and project group members helps organisations identify strengths and weaknesses in their change management processes and make informed decisions about necessary changes and improvements.

- The RATICA framework, which stands for Regularity, Actionability, Transparency, Inclusivity, Communication, and Accountability, can be used as a guide to incorporate key elements of continuous feedback into the change journey.

- Take into account the organisational context, including industry, size, structure, and external influences, when interpreting the data, as these factors can shape and influence the culture and its dynamics.

- Create a safe environment that encourages honest and open feedback.

- Encourage a culture of continuous learning and improvement by using the data analysis findings as a basis for reflection, discussion, and learning opportunities within the organisation.

CHAPTER 11: Step Four – Creative Concepts

Chapter pathway

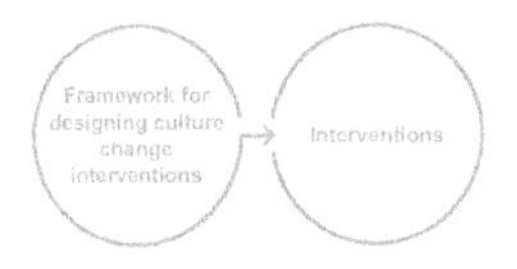

After delving into various aspects of organisational culture, including Collaborative Commitment, Cultural Compass, and Continuous Feedback in previous chapters, we are now ready to move to Step Four, to develop a culture change strategy.

A well-designed strategy serves as a roadmap for intentionally shaping an organisation's culture and bridging the gap between the current and desired state. It involves a systematic approach that includes identifying strengths and weaknesses, setting clear goals and objectives, defining desired cultural behaviours and attitudes, and establishing action plans for implementation.

A robust strategy considers the unique context and dynamics of the organisation, such as its industry, size, structure, and workforce. It serves as a guiding framework for leaders to align their efforts, engage employees, and drive sustainable cultural change throughout the organisation.

Creating a change strategy involves intentionally designing a plan to address any identified cultural gaps (as mentioned earlier in this book) and achieve the desired outcomes. Organisations need to carefully plan and execute their cultural transformation efforts to ensure alignment with their vision, mission, and values.

In this chapter, we will put the pieces together to create a roadmap for intentional cultural change that aligns with the organisation's vision, mission, and values, ultimately leading to a more positive and productive organisational culture.

Framework for designing culture change interventions

Companies may utilise various formats for their strategy documents, and the following topic areas can be customised to align with your organisation's unique requirements or serve as a source of inspiration for the content of your strategy. These areas include:

- Clearly define the desired cultural state and articulate the vision for the organisation's culture.

- Outline the specific outcomes and results the organisation aims to achieve through the change initiative.
- Identify the specific changes in behaviours, attitudes, and norms that need to be promoted or discouraged to align with the desired culture.
- Determine the necessary resources, such as budget, personnel, technology, and other assets, required to implement the change initiative successfully.
- Identify key stakeholders, such as leaders, employees, customers, and other relevant parties, and establish strategies for engaging and involving them in the change process.
- Develop a comprehensive communication strategy to effectively communicate the purpose, goals, and progress of the change initiative to all stakeholders.
- Outline strategies and tactics for managing resistance to change, addressing challenges, and ensuring smooth execution of the change effort.
- Establish metrics and feedback mechanisms to track progress, measure success, and make data-driven decisions throughout the change initiative.
- Identify potential risks and challenges and develop contingency plans to mitigate them and ensure readiness for unexpected situations.
- Plan for periodic review and adjustment of the culture change strategy based on feedback, results, and changing organisational needs.

By utilising a strategy template that encompasses these key areas, organisations can create a comprehensive plan for driving intentional culture change and achieving their desired cultural outcomes. For a draft strategy template please visit https://hrfusion.podia.com/shadow-cultures-bonuses or use the QR code.

Interventions

When you are creating your strategy and plan you will need to consider what interventions you will need, and in the following section, we will explore various interventions that can be employed to drive positive changes in your organisation culture. It's important to note that there are countless possible interventions to choose from. However, for the purposes of this book, I will highlight 20 to provide you with some idea of what is feasible.

In the context of organisational development and change management, intervention refers to a deliberate and planned action or strategy designed to bring about desired changes in an organisation or its culture. Interventions are purposeful interventions that aim to address specific challenges or issues and facilitate positive change.

Some popular (in no particular order) cultural interventions for organisations which you may wish to consider are:

1. **Organisational structure and system strategy**
   These encompass the formal arrangements and processes within an organisation that determine how tasks, responsibilities, and authority are distributed. They play a critical role in shaping the culture, behaviour, and performance of an organisation. Leaders and managers need to understand and manage the organisational structure and systems to effectively lead change and manage cultural transformation. This may involve revisiting the structure, redesigning systems and processes, and implementing new practices that align with the desired culture. By leveraging the

structure and systems of the organisation, leaders can create an enabling environment that fosters the desired cultural changes and drives organisational success.

2. **Leadership development programmes**
   These programmes focus on developing leadership skills and behaviours that align with the desired culture. They may include training, coaching, and mentoring for leaders at all levels of the organisation to enhance their ability to positively influence the culture.
3. **Employee training and development**
   Providing training and development opportunities for employees to enhance their skills, knowledge, and capabilities can help them align with the desired cultural values and behaviours. This may include workshops, seminars, online courses, and other learning opportunities.
4. **Employee engagement initiatives**
   Engaging employees through regular feedback channels, company-wide gatherings, surveys, and other initiatives can help create a culture of open communication, active engagement, and employee empowerment.
5. **Diversity, equity, and inclusion (DEI) programmes**
   These programmes promote diversity, equity, and inclusion in the workplace, fostering a culture that values and respects individual differences and promotes a sense of belonging among employees from diverse backgrounds.
6. **Employee recognition programmes**
   Implementing formal programmes that acknowledge and reward employees for their contributions, achievements, and adherence to cultural values can reinforce desired behaviours and attitudes, and boost employee morale.
7. **Clear expectations and accountability**
   Setting clear expectations for performance, behaviour, and adherence to cultural values and holding everyone

accountable for their actions and behaviours can help reinforce the desired culture and create a sense of ownership among employees.

8. **Change management strategies**
   Implementing change management strategies that include effective communication, stakeholder engagement, and support mechanisms can help manage the transition to a new culture and facilitate buy-in from employees.
9. **Collaborative and cross-functional initiatives**
   Encouraging collaboration and cross-functional initiatives that foster teamwork, knowledge sharing, and mutual support can create a culture of collaboration and innovation.
10. **Wellness and work-life balance programmes**
    Implementing programmes that promote employee well-being, work-life balance, and a healthy work environment can contribute to a positive culture that values the holistic well-being of employees.
11. **Role modelling by leaders**
    Leaders serve as role models by consistently exhibiting the desired behaviours, values, and attitudes that reflect the desired culture. This includes leading by example and actively promoting and reinforcing cultural changes.
12. **Values and beliefs**
    Clarify and reinforce the organisation's core values and beliefs and align them with the desired culture to guide decision-making, behaviour, and actions.
13. **Team building**
    Enhance team dynamics, collaboration, and cohesion through team-building exercises, workshops, and activities that promote mutual trust, respect, and accountability.

14. **Recruitment**

    Ensure that the recruitment processes align with the desired culture, including identifying and attracting candidates who are a good fit for the organisation, and providing a comprehensive orientation that introduces new employees to the culture and values of the organisation.

15. **Performance management**

    Incorporate the desired culture into the performance management process and policies, including setting performance expectations that align with the organisation, providing regular feedback, and recognising and rewarding behaviours that reflect the desired culture.

16. **Career development**

    Offer career development opportunities that align with the culture and provide employees with the necessary skills and knowledge to contribute to the change efforts, including training, mentoring, and coaching.

17. **Employee engagement and retention**

    Implement initiatives to enhance employee engagement and retention, such as creating a positive work environment, promoting employee involvement and ownership, and recognising and rewarding employees who contribute to the culture change efforts.

18. **Performance improvement plans**

    Develop performance improvement plans for employees who may need additional support in aligning with the desired culture, including providing coaching, mentoring, and feedback to help them understand and adopt the desired culture.

19. **Exit interviews**

    Conduct exit interviews to gather feedback from employees who are leaving the organisation to understand their perceptions of the culture and identify any areas that may need further attention in the change efforts.

20. **Onboarding and organisational socialisation**
Implement a comprehensive and tailored onboarding or organisational socialisation process to facilitate the integration of new employees into the organisation, enabling them to acquire the essential knowledge, skills, and behaviours needed to become productive and effective members of the organisation.

It's important to remember that cultural change is a continuous process and may require a combination of interventions tailored to the specific needs of your organisation. Regular evaluation and adjustment of interventions based on feedback and outcomes are crucial to ensure their effectiveness in driving the desired cultural changes. By intentionally and strategically implementing cultural interventions, organisations can create a positive and thriving culture that fosters employee engagement, productivity, and organisational success.

Your call to action

Whilst I don't advise implementing everything in the list above, which ones will support your organisation's culture change? When you implement your chosen strategies, remember to define the desired culture, set clear goals, identify specific changes needed, allocate resources, engage stakeholders, communicate effectively, manage resistance, track progress, identify risks, and adapt as needed. Take intentional action to create a positive and thriving organisational culture. Drive success through strategic culture change!

The key takeaways from this chapter are:

- A well-designed change strategy serves as a roadmap for intentionally shaping an organisation's culture and bridging the gap between the current and desired cultural state.

- A robust culture strategy considers the unique context and dynamics of the organisation, such as its industry, size, structure, and workforce.

- Developing a change strategy involves identifying cultural strengths and weaknesses, setting clear goals and objectives, defining desired cultural behaviours and attitudes, and establishing action plans for implementation.

- Organisations should carefully plan and execute their cultural transformation efforts to ensure alignment with their vision, mission, and values.

- A strategy template can be used to define the desired cultural state, set goals and objectives, identify the specific changes needed, allocate resources, engage stakeholders, develop a communication plan, manage change, monitor and evaluate progress, identify risks, and establish contingency plans.

- Interventions, such as changes in organisational structure and systems, leadership development programmes, employee training and development, employee engagement initiatives, diversity, equity, and inclusion programmes, employee recognition programmes, and setting clear expectations and accountability, can be used to drive positive changes in organisational culture.

- Organisations should regularly review and adapt their change strategy based on feedback, results, and changing organisational needs.
- Regular reviews allow for adjustments to the strategy based on evolving organisational needs, ensuring the cultural transformation remains relevant and impactful.

CHAPTER 12: Step Five – Coordinated Execution

Chapter pathway

Implementing a project plan traditionally involves putting the planned activities and strategies into action to achieve the project's goals and objectives. This is the phase where the project plan is executed, and the project team works collaboratively to complete the project tasks, monitor progress, and make necessary adjustments to ensure successful project delivery. In Step Five, I will explore how to effectively implement the various elements of your plan or strategy. Please note that some of the below has already been covered in the previous chapter, however I thought it important to cover it here as it's a vital part of implementation.

The implementation phase of this type of project plan typically involves several key steps, including:

- Clearly defining the roles and responsibilities of team members and stakeholders involved in the project and ensuring that everyone understands their respective tasks and deadlines.
- Allocating the necessary resources, such as budget, personnel, equipment, and materials, to support the project activities and ensure smooth execution.
- Performing the planned project tasks according to the defined timeline, milestones, and deliverables, and closely monitoring progress against the project plan.
- Monitoring the project's progress and performance, comparing actual results against planned targets, and making necessary adjustments to keep the project on track.
- Maintaining open and effective communication with all stakeholders, including team members, clients, vendors, and other relevant parties, to ensure alignment and manage expectations.
- Identifying and addressing potential risks and issues that may arise during project implementation and taking proactive measures to mitigate their impact on the project's success.
- Ensuring that project deliverables meet the defined quality standards and conducting quality assurance and control activities throughout the implementation phase.
- Managing any changes or modifications to the project plan that may arise during implementation, and ensuring that they are properly assessed, approved, and communicated to all relevant stakeholders.
- Keeping accurate records of project progress, milestones, and achievements, and providing regular reports to stakeholders on the project's status and performance.

» Addressing any problems, conflicts, or issues that may arise during project implementation, and finding effective solutions to keep the project on track.

Effective project implementation requires close monitoring, coordination, communication, and proactive management of resources, risks, quality, and changes. It is a critical phase of the project management process that ensures that the project plan is executed successfully, and the project's goals and objectives are achieved as planned.

Alternative approaches to change implementation

Unconventional project styles refer to unique or non-traditional approaches to managing and implementing projects. These styles may deviate from conventional or traditional project management methodologies and practices and may involve innovative, experimental, or creative techniques to achieve project goals and outcomes.

These styles often prioritise flexibility, adaptability, and collaboration, and may be well suited for complex or dynamic projects where traditional project management approaches may not be as effective. Some examples of unconventional project styles include:

Agile

Agile is a modern and dynamic project management approach that has gained popularity in recent years due to its flexibility, adaptability, and collaborative nature. Agile emphasises continuous improvement, customer satisfaction, and iterative progress, making it well suited for fast-paced, complex, and uncertain environments.

In this approach, cross-functional teams work closely together, frequently collaborate with stakeholders, and regularly adapt their plans and strategies based on feedback and changing requirements. Agile promotes a mindset of flexibility, experimentation, and learning, allowing teams to respond quickly to changes and deliver value incrementally.

Positives of agile project management:

- Emphasises adaptability and flexibility, enabling teams to respond to changes in requirements, priorities, and market conditions for faster delivery and increased customer satisfaction.
- Promotes collaboration and active involvement of team members, stakeholders, and customers, fostering transparency, communication, and shared ownership.
- Uses a repeated approach for continuous feedback and learning, allowing for faster issue resolution and adjustments as needed.
- Focuses on delivering value incrementally, resulting in faster time-to-market and customer-aligned outcomes.

Negatives of agile project management:

- Less predictability due to frequent changes in requirements and priorities, making it challenging to estimate timelines and resources.
- Requires a mindset shift and changes in traditional practices, leading to a learning curve for some teams.
- Demands active participation throughout the project, which may be resource-intensive for some organisations.
- The flexible nature can lead to scope creep if not managed properly.

» Prioritises functional deliverables over exhaustive documentation, which may not align with some organisations' standards.

It's important to carefully consider the specific needs and characteristics of a project and the organisation's readiness for agile before adopting this approach. Proper training, planning, and implementation can help mitigate the challenges and leverage the benefits of agile to achieve successful project outcomes.

Scrum

Scrum is a widely used agile framework for project management that provides a structured approach for developing complex products. It is particularly popular in software development but can also be applied to other industries and domains. Scrum is based on the principles of transparency, inspection, and adaptation, and promotes collaboration, flexibility, and customer-centricity.

In scrum, work is organised into small, cross-functional teams that work collaboratively to deliver value in short timeframes known as sprints. Scrum teams are self-organising and empowered, with the Product Owner responsible for defining the product backlog (i.e., the prioritised list of work) and the Development Team responsible for delivering the product incrementally. The Scrum Master serves as a facilitator, coach, and servant leader, ensuring that the team follows the scrum framework and continuously improves.

This method follows a time-boxed approach, with a set of predefined events, roles, and artefacts that provide structure to the project. The key events in scrum include Sprint, Sprint Planning, Daily Scrum, Sprint Review, and Sprint

Retrospective, which promote collaboration, transparency, and continuous improvement. The artefacts in scrum include the Product Backlog, Sprint Backlog, and Increment, which provide visibility into the work and progress of the project.

A key focus with scrum is on delivering value incrementally, allowing for fast feedback, learning, and adaptation. It encourages continuous improvement and adaptation based on feedback from stakeholders and customers. Scrum promotes a culture of transparency, where progress, challenges, and risks are made visible, enabling timely decision-making and problem-solving.

Overall, scrum offers a flexible and collaborative approach to project management, allowing teams to be agile and responsive to changing requirements and market conditions. It provides a framework for iterative and incremental development, promoting transparency, inspection, and adaptation to achieve successful project outcomes.

Positives of scrum project management:

» Allows for flexibility and adaptability, enabling faster delivery and improved customer satisfaction.

» Promotes collaboration, transparency, and teamwork, leading to better decision-making and improved project outcomes.

» Delivers value incrementally in short sprints, advantageous in dynamic industries or competitive markets.

» Emphasises customer satisfaction and feedback for higher retention rates and customer-aligned projects.

» Fosters a culture of continuous improvement through retrospectives, leading to optimised performance over time.

Negatives of scrum project management:

- Requires a mindset shift and a learning curve for teams new to scrum.
- Less predictability due to changing requirements, requiring frequent adjustments.
- Demands significant time and effort from team members and stakeholders.
- Flexible nature can lead to scope creep without proper management.
- Relies heavily on self-organising and empowered teams, which may pose challenges if not fully capable.

It's important to carefully consider the specific needs and characteristics of a project and the organisation's readiness for scrum before adopting it as a project management approach. Proper training, coaching, and implementation can help mitigate the challenges and leverage the benefits of scrum to achieve successful project outcomes.

Lean project management

Lean project management is an approach that focuses on maximising customer value while minimising waste in project execution. It is inspired by the principles of lean thinking, which originated in manufacturing but has since been applied to various industries, including project management. Lean project management emphasises efficiency, effectiveness, and continuous improvement to deliver high-quality results with minimum waste of resources.

Lean project management is based on several core principles, including the following.

Value

The central objective of lean project management is to deliver meaningful value to the customer or end user. This entails comprehending and aligning with customer requirements and expectations while tailoring project goals and deliverables accordingly.

Waste reduction

The core principle of lean project management is to identify and eliminate waste during project execution, which may include redundant processes, activities, or resources that do not contribute value to the customer. This encompasses minimising rework, delays, defects, and other forms of waste that can hinder project efficiency and effectiveness.

Continuous improvement

Fostering a culture of continuous improvement, the principles of lean project management advocate for regular reflection on team performance and proactive pursuit of opportunities to optimise processes, practices, and outcomes. Data, metrics, and feedback are leveraged to identify areas for refinement and implement changes aimed at achieving superior results.

Team empowerment

A key focus of lean project management is to empower teams to make decisions and take ownership of their work. This includes fostering a collaborative, accountable, and autonomous environment among team members while nurturing a culture of trust and innovation.

Visual management

Lean project management encourages visualising project progress, status, and performance to provide transparency and promote effective communication. This may involve visual boards, charts, or other tools that allow team members and stakeholders to quickly understand the project's status and make informed decisions.

Just-in-time delivery

A core principle of lean project management is to deliver work just-in-time, or as close to the actual need as possible, to minimise unnecessary delays, inventory, or overproduction. This entails optimising workflows, reducing dependencies, and ensuring that work is delivered precisely when it is most needed, resulting in improved efficiency and effectiveness in project execution.

Lean project management can be applied to various project types and sizes, including both traditional and agile projects. It emphasises efficiency, effectiveness, and customer value while promoting continuous improvement and empowering teams. By eliminating waste and focusing on value, lean project management aims to optimise project outcomes and deliver results that meet or exceed customer expectations.

Positives of lean project management

- Identifies and eliminates waste for improved efficiency and productivity.
- Emphasises customer needs for higher satisfaction and loyalty.
- Cultivates a culture of continuous improvement, leading to better project results over time.
- Empowers teams for increased accountability, autonomy, and innovation.
- Focuses on visual management and effective communication for transparency and better collaboration.

Negatives of lean project management

- Requires a mindset shift and a learning curve for teams new to lean.
- Less flexibility compared to agile in rapidly changing environments.

- Resource-intensive for implementing practices like visual management and continuous improvement.
- Relying on data and metrics can be challenging without adequate capabilities.
- May not suit projects with unique or complex requirements.

As with any project management approach, lean project management has its positives and negatives. It can be effective in improving project efficiency, customer value, and team engagement, but it may also require a learning curve, and resource investment, and may not be suitable for all projects. It's important to carefully consider the specific needs and characteristics of a project and the organisation's readiness for lean project management before adopting it as a project management approach. Proper training, coaching, and implementation can effectively address the challenges and capitalise on the advantages of lean project management, leading to successful project outcomes.

Design thinking

Design thinking project management is an approach that combines the principles and practices of design thinking with project management methodologies to solve complex problems, generate innovative ideas, and deliver successful projects. Design thinking is a human-centred, iterative approach to problem-solving that involves empathy, experimentation, and iteration, while project management is a structured approach to planning, executing, and controlling projects. Design thinking project management integrates these two approaches to create a collaborative, user-centric, and iterative process for managing projects.

The key principles of a design thinking project management include the following.

Human-centred approach

Placing the needs and perspectives of end-users, stakeholders, and team members at the forefront, project management with a human-centred approach involves empathising with users, understanding their needs and pain points, and designing solutions that meet their expectations and deliver value.

Iterative and experimental mindset

Encouraging experimentation and iteration to continuously improve solutions and adapt to changing requirements, project management with an iterative and experimental mindset involves testing and validating ideas through prototypes, feedback loops, and rapid iterations to refine and optimise project outcomes.

Collaborative and cross-functional team

Promoting collaboration and diversity of perspectives, project management with a focus on collaborative and cross-functional teams involves bringing together team members with diverse skills, backgrounds, and expertise to foster creativity, innovation, and problem-solving.

Visual and tangible representations

Utilising visual and tangible representations, such as sketches, diagrams, and prototypes, to communicate ideas, facilitate discussions, and co-create solutions, project management with visual and tangible representations helps align team members, stakeholders, and users around a shared understanding of the project's goals and outcomes.

Flexibility and adaptability

Recognising that projects are dynamic and require flexibility and adaptability, project management with a focus on flexibility and adaptability involves being open to change, embracing uncertainty, and adjusting plans and solutions as new insights emerge throughout the project lifecycle.

User feedback and validation

Emphasising the importance of user feedback and validation, project management with a focus on user feedback and validation involves actively seeking feedback from users, incorporating it into the iterative process, and validating solutions through user testing and checking to ensure that they meet user needs and expectations.

Application to various project types

Project management with a human-centred, iterative, collaborative, and flexible approach can be applied to various project types, ranging from product development to process improvement to organisational change.

Design thinking involves a collaborative and iterative approach to problem-solving, with a strong focus on understanding user needs, experimentation, and adaptation. By combining these principles with project management methodologies, this approach aims to deliver innovative, user-centric, and successful project outcomes.

Positives of design thinking project management:

- Prioritises end-users' and stakeholders' needs for valuable solutions.
- Encourages creativity and innovation among team members.
- Promotes collaboration for a diverse range of ideas and solutions.
- Allows for continuous improvement and adaptation throughout the project lifecycle.

- » Emphasises user feedback and validation for effective and relevant solutions.
- » Flexible and adaptable to changing project requirements.

Negatives of design thinking project management:

- » Subjective nature may result in biased solutions based on personal opinions.
- » The repeated process can be time-consuming and impact project timelines.
- » Uncertainty in outcomes due to experimentation.
- » Requires additional resources to support the collaborative process.
- » Resistance from team members and stakeholders to the cultural shift.
- » The lack of a structured framework may require additional planning and organisation.

It's important to note that the positives and negatives of design thinking project management may vary depending on the specific context and implementation of the approach. Organisations should carefully consider the unique characteristics of their projects and teams when deciding to adopt design thinking project management practices.

Your call to action

Take decisive action! Evaluate project characteristics to grasp the scope and impact of cultural change. Define clear requirements and goals aligned with your organisation's vision.

Choose the best project management approach. Craft a comprehensive implementation plan with precise steps and milestones. Establish roles and responsibilities, ensuring everyone knows their contributions. Allocate resources wisely.

Nurture collaboration and communication within your team. Embrace adaptability to overcome unexpected challenges. Monitor progress diligently. Learn from experiences by gathering feedback and conducting reviews to enhance future projects. Implement these steps consistently for successful outcomes and continuous improvement. Act now!

The key takeaways in this chapter include:

- Effective project implementation requires close monitoring, coordination, communication, and proactive management of resources, risks, quality, and changes.
- Unconventional project styles refer to unique or non-traditional approaches to managing and implementing projects, such as agile, scrum, lean project management, and design thinking project management.
- Agile is a flexible and collaborative approach that emphasises continuous improvement, customer satisfaction, and iterative progress, making it well suited for fast-paced, complex, and uncertain environments.
- Scrum is a widely used agile framework that provides a structured approach for developing complex products, based on principles of transparency, inspection, and adaptation.
- Lean project management focuses on maximising customer value while minimising waste in project execution, emphasising efficiency, effectiveness, and continuous improvement.
- Design thinking project management combines the principles of design thinking with project management methodologies to solve complex problems, generate innovative ideas, and deliver successful projects in a user-centric and iterative manner.

- It's important to carefully consider the specific needs and characteristics of a project and the organisation's readiness before adopting unconventional project styles, and proper training, coaching, and implementation can help mitigate challenges and leverage the benefits of these approaches.

- Each project style has its positives and negatives, and organisations should carefully consider the unique context and implementation of these approaches to determine their suitability for their projects and teams.

CHAPTER 13: Step Six – Constant Assessment

Chapter pathway

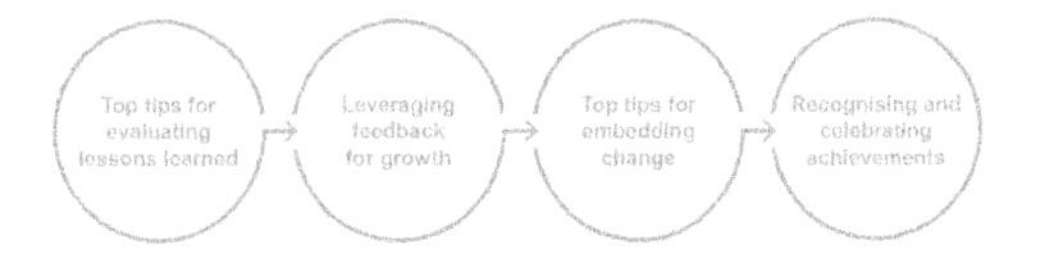

As projects move towards the implementation phase, Step Six, it's typical for companies to start looking ahead to the next project. However, it's vital not to neglect the significance of evaluating the achievements, lessons learned, and areas for enhancement of the current project before moving on.

Furthermore, it's crucial to have a well-defined strategy for integrating the positive changes that have already been made and fostering continuous improvement. This chapter centres on the concluding phase of the Cultural Change Programme, which entails embedding and assessing the changes that have been accomplished thus far and establishing a foundation for ongoing improvement.

Top tips for evaluating lessons learned

Evaluating project lessons learned is another crucial process that allows organisations to identify and capture insights, best practices, and recommendations from completed projects. Here are some top tips for effectively evaluating project lessons learned:

- Create a safe and non-judgemental environment where project team members and stakeholders feel comfortable sharing their feedback, insights, and lessons learned. Encourage open and honest communication to capture a comprehensive range of perspectives.
- Review project documentation, including project plans, reports, meeting minutes, and other relevant documents, to identify lessons learned from the project. Look for areas where improvements could have been made or where successes could be replicated in future projects.
- Conduct post-project evaluations to assess the project's performance against established success criteria and objectives. Use these evaluations as an opportunity to reflect on what worked well and what could have been done differently for better outcomes.
- Involve all relevant stakeholders, including project team members, sponsors, customers, and end-users, in the evaluation process. Collect feedback from different perspectives to gain a comprehensive understanding of project lessons learned.

- Follow a structured approach to evaluating project lessons learned. Use established evaluation methodologies, such as root cause analysis, SWOT analysis, or after-action reviews, to systematically identify, analyse, and document lessons learned.
- Capture both project successes and failures as valuable lessons learned. Celebrate successes and acknowledge failures as opportunities for improvement. Learning from both successes and failures can help drive continuous improvement in future projects.
- Document the lessons learned from the evaluation process in a systematic and organised manner. Share these lessons learned with relevant stakeholders and make them accessible for future reference. This can help prevent the repetition of mistakes and promote best practices in future projects.
- Use the insights gained from evaluating project lessons learned to update and improve organisational processes, procedures, and project management practices. Incorporate the lessons learned into standard operating procedures to ensure that the knowledge gained is institutionalised and applied in future projects.
- Identify and prioritise action items based on the lessons learned from the evaluation process. Follow up on these action items to ensure that they are implemented and integrated into future projects.
- Continuously review and improve the lessons learned process in your organisation. Solicit feedback from stakeholders, assess the effectiveness of the process, and make adjustments as needed to enhance the capture and utilisation of project lessons learned.

By following these top tips for evaluating project lessons learned, organisations can effectively capture valuable insights, best practices, and recommendations from completed projects, and use them to drive continuous improvement in future projects for better project outcomes.

Leveraging feedback for growth

Evaluating project successes and failures can provide valuable insights for organisations to create meaningful improvements. While successes are often celebrated, failures are equally important as they offer opportunities for learning and growth. By leveraging both successes and failures, organisations can drive continuous improvement and achieve better project outcomes.

Successes provide valuable examples of what has worked well in a project, showcasing best practices, effective strategies, and successful outcomes. Organisations can analyse and replicate these successes in future projects to achieve similar results. Successes can be used as benchmarks to set higher standards and raise the bar for future projects. Celebrating successes and recognising team members' contributions can also boost morale and motivation, encouraging a culture of excellence and innovation.

On the other hand, failures offer valuable opportunities for reflection, analysis, and improvement. Failures can reveal areas where the project fell short, highlight mistakes or missteps, and identify areas for improvement. Organisations can conduct root cause analysis to understand the underlying reasons for failures and use them as lessons learned to prevent similar mistakes in future projects. Failures can also stimulate creativity and innovation by encouraging teams to think differently and explore alternative approaches.

Combining successes and failures in the evaluation process can create a well-rounded perspective on project performance. By analysing both the positives and negatives, organisations can gain a holistic view of the project's strengths, weaknesses, opportunities, and threats. This can inform decision-making, strategic planning, and resource allocation for future projects.

Furthermore, using both successes and failures to drive continuous improvement can create a culture of learning and growth within the organisation. It encourages team members to embrace a growth mindset, where failures are seen as opportunities for improvement rather than as reasons for blame or punishment. It fosters a collaborative and inclusive environment where team members are encouraged to share their successes and failures openly, facilitating knowledge sharing and organisational learning.

> Combining successes and failures in the evaluation process can create a well-rounded perspective on project performance.

Top tips for embedding change

Embedding change in an organisation can be a complex and challenging process. Here are some top tips to help you effectively embed change:

- A clear and compelling vision is essential in guiding the change effort. Ensure that the vision is communicated consistently throughout the organisation and that it aligns with the desired culture.

- Great cultural change cannot be imposed from the top down. It requires the active involvement and engagement of employees at all levels of the organisation. Create opportunities for employees to provide input, feedback, and suggestions, and involve them in the decision-making process to foster ownership and commitment to the new culture.
- Align organisational systems, processes, and policies: change should not be limited to just changing behaviours or attitudes, but also aligning organisational systems, processes, and policies with the desired culture. Review and adapt existing systems, processes, and policies to ensure they are consistent with the new culture and support its sustainability.
- Leadership plays a crucial role in change efforts. Leaders should model the behaviours and actions that reflect the desired culture. Be visible, accessible, and approachable, and demonstrate the values and norms through your own actions.
- Change may require employees to acquire new skills, knowledge, and behaviours. Provide ongoing training and development opportunities to support employees in adapting to the new culture and building the necessary capabilities to thrive in the changed environment.
- Effective communication is vital in change efforts. Be transparent about the reasons for the change, the progress, and the expected outcomes. Communicate consistently through various channels, such as company-wide gatherings, newsletters, and regular updates, to keep employees informed and engaged.
- Celebrate and recognise the progress and achievements of individuals and teams who are exemplifying the new culture. This reinforces the desired behaviours and creates positive momentum towards embedding the new culture.

- Regularly evaluate the effectiveness of the change efforts using clear and measurable metrics. Collect feedback from employees, monitor progress, and make adjustments as needed. Continuously adapt and refine the change strategy based on evaluation findings.

> Great cultural change cannot be imposed from the top down. It requires the active involvement and engagement of employees at all levels of the organisation.

- Embed a culture of continuous improvement that encourages employees to seek feedback, learn from mistakes, and continuously strive for better outcomes. Embrace a growth mindset that recognises that change is an ongoing journey that requires constant learning and improvement.
- Embedding change takes time and effort. It requires patience, persistence, and resilience to navigate challenges and setbacks along the way. Stay committed to the vision and the desired culture and be persistent in driving the change effort forward.

By following these top tips, organisations can increase the likelihood of successfully embedding change and creating a new culture that is aligned with their strategic objectives and values.

Recognising and celebrating achievements

Lastly in this chapter, I would like to talk about an area often forgotten that is a crucial and non-negotiable aspect to establish and maintain an outstanding work environment: consistently recognising and celebrating achievements. This is an essential action that cannot be overlooked if you genuinely aspire to create a positive workplace culture. To help get you started with this, here are some fantastic ways to celebrate successes in the workplace:

Acknowledge and appreciate the efforts and achievements of your team members in a public and meaningful way. This can be done through verbal praise, written notes, or public announcements.

Provide rewards or incentives such as bonuses, gift cards, or extra time off as a way of recognising and celebrating successes. This not only shows appreciation but also motivates employees to continue their good work.

Organise team celebrations or gatherings to commemorate successes. This can be in the form of team lunches, happy hours, or special events to acknowledge achievements and boost team morale.

Share success stories and achievements of team members in organisation-wide communications, such as newsletters, internal blogs, or social media platforms. This showcases their accomplishments and encourages a culture of celebration and recognition.

Tailor your recognition and celebrations to the individual preferences and interests of team members. Some may prefer public recognition, while others may appreciate a private word of thanks or a small, personalised gift.

Offer professional development opportunities such as training programmes, workshops, or conferences as a way to celebrate achievements and invest in the growth and development of your team members.

Granting flexible work arrangements as a reward for a job well done can be an excellent way to celebrate successes and show appreciation for the hard work and dedication of your team.

Remember, the key is to make celebrations genuine, frequent, and inclusive so that all team members feel valued and motivated to continue their efforts towards success.

Your call to action

Start with the end in mind; positive change requires constant assessment. Make time to evaluate project achievements and lessons learned, document and share insights, leverage successes and failures for improvement, embed change in your organisation, recognise and celebrate achievements, foster collaboration and cross-functional teamwork, and continuously monitor and enhance.

There are lots of top tips in this chapter to help you take action now to cultivate a culture of learning and growth.

The key takeaways in this chapter include:

- It's vital not to neglect the significance of evaluating the achievements, lessons learned, and areas for enhancement of the current project before moving on to the next one.
- Follow a structured approach to evaluating project lessons learned, involving all relevant stakeholders, and capturing both successes and failures as valuable lessons learned.
- Use both successes and failures to drive continuous improvement and foster a culture of learning and growth within the organisation.
- Embedding change requires a clear and compelling vision, active involvement and engagement of employees, alignment of organisational systems and processes, effective communication, monitoring progress, addressing resistance, and being patient and persistent.
- The key to effective recognition and celebration is to make it genuine, frequent, and inclusive so that all team members feel valued and motivated to continue their efforts towards success. Celebrating achievements not only boosts morale and motivation but also creates a positive work culture that fosters growth and success.
- To establish a culture of learning and growth, you need to foster continuous improvement and drive cultural change; organisations should create a culture that encourages learning and growth.

- Recognising and appreciating the efforts and achievements of employees is essential for creating a positive workplace culture. Organisations should implement practices and initiatives that celebrate and acknowledge individual and team accomplishments.

- In cultural change efforts, it is essential to promote collaboration and foster cross-functional teamwork. Breaking down silos and encouraging employees from different departments and levels to work together can lead to greater innovation, problem-solving, and a shared sense of ownership in achieving the desired cultural change.

CHAPTER 14: Recipe for Success – Conclusion

You may be wondering how you can implement this process within your organisation. So before I tell you how I can support you, I'd like to share a real-life case study to show how I have used these six steps within a company seeking culture change.

Introduction

This case study presents a live example of a total reward project undertaken by a housing association, with large care and support services, employing approximately 1,300 employees located in a variety of locations across the UK to support its growth and navigate significant changes. The project aimed to attract and retain top talent while ensuring fairness in terms and conditions. Led by myself and two HR and reward experts each heading up various aspects of this project, the project followed my structured six-step approach to achieve its objectives successfully.

To give you some background, over the five years prior to this intervention, the organisation underwent substantial growth and transformation, including a company-wide restructure and the integration of another company into its group. To address the organisation's talent management and fairness concerns, the project team initiated a total reward project.

Step One – Collaborative Commitment

We initiated this project by promoting collaboration and establishing a shared vision to drive cultural change. The project team actively involved key stakeholders, including boards, executives, directors, and employees, in order to grasp their desired outcomes, timeframes, budgetary considerations, and aspirations for cultural change.

In order to ensure we challenged any biases we enlisted the help of the company equity, diversity and inclusion working group and an external reward consultant.

Numerous meetings, working groups, and consultations were conducted to ensure comprehensive engagement and using listening to understand techniques to clarify our understanding, where helpful, in ensuring we understood people's views. To formalise the project's direction, a guiding principles document was created, thoroughly reviewed by the project team, directors, and executives, and eventually approved by the group board and its chairperson. Although at this stage there were no challenges, there was concern among colleagues that this was a cost-cutting exercise and that they would lose pay or rewards. However, by fostering open and honest communication we were able to assure colleagues that it was not a cost-cutting exercise but instead a harmonisation of all the company's terms and conditions. This collaborative commitment laid a robust foundation for the project's success.

Step Two – Cultural Compass

In this step, the project team conducted a comprehensive analysis of the organisation's existing culture and identified areas for improvement. We employed various methods, including colleague workshops, attended various team meetings, conducted surveys, obtained external benchmarking from a reward consultant, and networked and researched other companies' reward packages. In addition to this, we collected various finance data and created a project plan using a Gantt chart.

One of the things we did that worked really well was listing all the current terms and conditions and benefits colleagues received and asking them to individually put them in their own personal priority order. Once we received them all back, we were able to review them against the company values and the overall guiding principles for this project. This then helped in the consultation process that followed. Continuous feedback from stakeholders ensured that the project stayed on track and aligned with the desired cultural transformation. This step served as an ongoing litmus test to gauge progress.

Step Three – Continuous Feedback

To ensure accountability and minimise bias, the project team established a feedback mechanism involving employees, customers, and other stakeholders which consisted of a communication and engagement plan. This plan included creating a feedback loop between colleagues, leadership, and the board. In order to do this we set up a calendar of events, presentations and reports, and attended regular meetings and workshops, in addition to arranging days with directors and executive directors, presenting and attending committee and board meetings, then ensuring updates were fed back to employees for their views.

This iterative process allowed for diverse perspectives and helped maintain alignment with stakeholders' expectations.

Step Four – Creative Concepts

Based on the strong relationships established with stakeholders and the data collected, the project team identified priority areas and designed phases for the total reward project. These covered the following areas:

Phase one focused on aligning contractual terms and conditions, what we went on to call core benefits, including working hours, holiday pay, sickness entitlement, and notice periods. Transparent communication and evidence-based information facilitated discussions with staff forums, ensuring understanding and acceptance of decisions.

Phase two addressed company cars and additional benefits, while phase three focused on pay and recognition, in adherence to the agreed terms of reference.

Using the terms and conditions and benefits list that colleagues completed (as referred to in Step Two) we asked them to tell us what they would like to see offered, maybe what other companies do or benefits that would help them, obviously including a strong caveat that we would not be able to do everything. This gave us some great ideas and allowed us to see how things like the sickness offer needed to change.

Step Five – Coordinated Execution

With an agreed-upon phased approach, the project plan we created had a detailed implementation, ensuring timeframes were manageable, we had identified the accountable person and the responsible person for each element, and also considering key meetings, workshops, and foreseeable events.

However, the project faced unforeseen challenges when the global pandemic emerged near the end of phase one. Nevertheless, by adapting and leveraging the previous steps, the team managed to adjust the project's timeline and ensure continued progress.

Step Six – Constant Assessment

The final step focused on evaluating progress and embedding cultural change within the organisation. Regular assessments were conducted to identify areas for improvement and ensure the long-term sustainability of the new ways of working. The organisation's investment of time, effort, and resources in this project highlighted the importance of evaluating, learning, and adapting to achieve lasting results. However, one of the biggest lessons to be learnt from this project was the time it took to complete: what started as a one-year project soon became a three-year one. This was mainly due to people's availability to attend meetings and workshops, the pandemic, and following a traditional Gantt chart approach to project management which in hindsight was not the best approach for this project.

Conclusion

By following a structured six-step programme, the organisation successfully implemented the total reward project, overcoming challenges and achieving its objectives. The collaborative commitment, cultural analysis, continuous feedback, creative concepts, coordinated execution, and constant assessment ensured the project's effectiveness and recognition. The project's ability to adapt and engage stakeholders contributed to its overall success, setting a strong foundation for continued organisational transformation with a strong ethical culture. This project was also externally recognised by being shortlisted for three Personnel Today awards for: HR Impact, Employee Experience and Change Management.

The last word

Companies that follow this structured six-step Cultural Change Programme can significantly increase their chances of achieving long-lasting and impactful change within their organisation. Each stage in the programme plays a critical role in the overall success of the change effort, with the final stage of embedding and evaluating being particularly crucial.

In summary, the first step in the programme, **Collaborative Commitment**, involves gaining buy-in and commitment from all levels of the organisation. This step emphasises the importance of engaging employees in the change process from the beginning, fostering ownership and shared responsibility for the desired culture. When employees are actively involved and committed to the change, they are more likely to embrace and sustain the new culture.

Cultural Compass is the second step, which involves conducting a thorough analysis of the current culture and identifying its strengths and weaknesses. This step helps organisations gain a clear understanding of their existing culture and its impact on their performance and outcomes. It also provides insights into the cultural elements that need to be changed to align with the desired culture.

Continuous Feedback is the third step in the programme, emphasising the importance of ongoing monitoring and feedback to assess the progress of the change effort. Regular analysis and feedback allow organisations to make data-driven decisions, identify areas that may require adjustments, and ensure that the change effort stays on track. This step helps organisations stay agile and responsive to the evolving needs and dynamics of the organisation and its culture.

Creative Concepts form the fourth step, involving the development and implementation of creative strategies and interventions to drive change. This step may involve training programmes, leadership development initiatives, process improvements, and other innovative approaches tailored to the specific needs of the organisation. Innovative interventions help organisations disrupt old patterns and behaviours and facilitate the adoption of new cultural norms and practices.

The fifth step, **Coordinated Execution,** is the execution of the change plan. This step involves rolling out the planned interventions and strategies across the organisation and ensuring that they are effectively implemented. Proper implementation requires careful planning, coordination, and communication to ensure that the change efforts are embraced by employees and integrated into the organisation's day-to-day operations.

Finally, the sixth and crucial step is **Constant Assessment**. Embedding involves integrating the new culture into the organisation's systems, processes, policies, and practices, and making it a part of the organisational DNA. This step requires sustained efforts to ensure that the change becomes deeply ingrained in the organisation's culture and remains sustainable over the long term.

Evaluating is equally important in this stage, as it involves regularly assessing the effectiveness of the change effort using objective metrics and feedback from employees. Evaluation helps organisations identify any gaps, challenges, or areas for improvement, and make necessary adjustments to ensure that the change effort continues to yield the desired outcomes.

Embedding everything in the organisation, from the change plan to the interventions, feedback mechanisms, and evaluation processes, is crucial for long-lasting change. It ensures that the change effort becomes ingrained in the organisational fabric, guiding behaviours, decisions, and actions across all levels of the organisation. When change is embedded and evaluated, it becomes a sustainable part of the organisation's culture, driving performance, innovation, and success over the long term.

In conclusion, the six-step Cultural Change Programme emphasises the importance of a systematic and holistic approach to change. From gaining collaborative commitment to understanding the existing culture, implementing innovative interventions, and continuous analysis and feedback, to embedding and evaluating the change effort, each stage plays a crucial role in achieving long-lasting and impactful cultural change within organisations. By following this programme and prioritising the embedding and evaluating stage, organisations can increase the chances of successfully transforming their culture and achieving sustainable change.

What's next?

As we come to the end of this book, I want to emphasise that this is just the beginning of your change story. Now is the time for decisive action to drive positive change and achieve better outcomes for leaders, employees, and your organisation as a whole.

Throughout this book, I have shed light on the shadow culture that exists within our organisations and teams. Drawing from my personal experiences and years of knowledge, I have provided you with a tool that can help us transform our culture for the better.

Now, armed with the information from this book, it is up to you to choose your next steps. You can follow the model from start to finish or select specific elements that suit your current needs. It's okay if you need to revisit certain aspects of the model; this tool is meant to be used in a way that best serves you and your organisation.

With dedication and perseverance, you have the power to shape a thriving and innovative organisational culture, where individuals can truly flourish. And if you find that you need support in implementing the principles discussed in this book. I invite you to visit my website, hr-fusion.co.uk where you can find my contact details.

Don't forget you can download some complimentary resources here https://hrfusion.podia.com/shadow-cultures-bonuses.

By working together, we can create a customised approach that addresses the specific challenges and goals of your organisation. From conducting culture audits and developing change strategies to providing ongoing support and guidance, I am here to assist you in creating a thriving and innovative organisational culture.

Thank you for embarking on this transformative journey with me. Together, let's make a difference and shape workplaces where individuals can be their best selves and find happiness at work.

ABOUT THE AUTHOR

Rachel is a strategic and authentic HR leader with over 20 years of experience in the field of HR and organisational development. Throughout her career, she has successfully overseen significant structural and cultural change initiatives, consistently finding strategic solutions to enhance employee experience and improve organisational performance.

Rachel possesses a diverse portfolio of expertise, including strategic HR, total reward management, mergers and acquisitions, championing equality, diversity, and inclusion, employee health and well-being, change management, collaborative working, learning and development, talent management, workforce planning, excellence through data analysis, and employee engagement. Her commitment to continuous learning is reflected in her three postgraduate qualifications in Reward Management, Psychology of Organisational Development, and Human Resources.

Leveraging her extensive experience and drawing insights from other change leaders, Rachel provides readers with valuable perspectives on different organisational cultures. She also offers a method for diagnosing these cultures, empowering readers to take actionable steps towards cultural change within their own organisations.

Integrity is the foundation of Rachel's work ethic, which she has demonstrated throughout her career dedicated to personal growth, building strong relationships, and achieving success. Her valuable life and work experiences, combined with her strong educational background, contribute to her effectiveness as a strategic HR leader.

Rachel's accomplishments and unwavering commitment to positive change make her a valuable asset in the field of strategic HR leadership. Her consultancy, HR Fusion Ltd, was established to provide tailored solutions, strategic guidance, and practical tools to organisations seeking transformation. Through HR Fusion, Rachel bridges the gap between theory and practice, empowering businesses to unlock their full potential, foster thriving work cultures, and achieve sustainable success.

Guided by her belief in the transformative power of culture change, Rachel aspires to guide organisations towards sustainable growth and engaged employees. Through personalised consulting services, she leverages her expertise and commitment to support organisations on their journey to success.

REFERENCES

1 Alex Chesterfield (FCA), Dr Tom Reader (London School of Economics) and Dr Alex Gillespie (London School of Economics), 2019. "Measuring culture – can it be done?" FCA Insight, 4 September 2019, https://www.fca.org.uk/insight/measuring-culture-can-it-be-done

2 E.H. Schein, 2010. *Organisational Culture and Leadership*, 4th ed., The Jossey-Bass business & management series, Jossey-Bass, San Francisco.

3 Ibid, p18.

4 Chris Dyer, 2018. *The Power of Company Culture: How any business can build a culture that improves productivity, performance and profits*, Kogan Page, p106.

5 Simon Sinek, 2014. *Leaders Eat Last: Why Some Teams Pull Together and Others Don't*, Portfolio/Penguin, New York, New York, p163.

6 Baroness Casey of Blackstock DBE CB, 2023. An independent review into the standards of behaviour and internal culture of the Metropolitan Police Service.

7 Cabinet Secretary, 2022. Findings Of Second Permanent Secretary's Investigation Into Alleged

Gatherings On Government Premises During Covid Restrictions.

8 Authority of the House of Commons, 2022. Post Office and Horizon – Compensation: interim report. Eighth Report of Session 2021–22.

9 Alex Chesterfield (FCA), Dr Tom Reader (London School of Economics) and Dr Alex Gillespie (London School of Economics), 2019. "Measuring culture – can it be done?" FCA Insight, https://www.fca.org.uk/insight/measuring-culture-can-it-be-done

10 Matthew Corritore, Amir Goldberg, and Sameer B. Srivastava, "The New Analytics of Culture: What email, Slack, and Glassdoor reveal about your organization", *Harvard Business Review Magazine*, Jan – Feb 2020, https://hbr.org/2020/01/the-new-analytics-of-culture

INDEX

Accountability, 13, 28, 32, 39–41, 43–44, 48, 51, 56, 73, 75, 79, 85, 89, 91–92, 98, 101–102, 131, 164–165, 167, 175–176, 180, 189, 211
Actionability, 164, 167, 169
Adaptive culture, 13
Agile, 30, 53, 63, 183–186, 189, 195, 215
Anchoring bias, 124, 133
Aspiration, 25
Autocratic leaders, 20
Availability bias, 123, 133
Building ownership, 104, 127–128, 134
Career development, 177
Case study: Metropolitan Police Service, 86–87
Case study: the Partygate scandal, 87–89
Case study: the Post Office scandal, 89–91
Change management strategies, 176
Clear expectations and accountability, 175, 180
Collaborating with leaders and stakeholders, 110, 112
Collaborative and cross-functional initiatives, 176
Collaborative culture, 12, 47–49, 66
Communicating findings and recommendations, 161
Communication, 11–12, 18, 20–21, 25–29, 31–33, 47–48, 55–57, 75–76, 92, 97–98, 102–103, 122, 124–125, 129, 131, 142, 144–145, 163–164, 166, 198, 202, 210, 212
Comparative analysis, 161, 168
Compliance culture, 73
Confirmation bias, 122, 133
Content analysis, 150, 160, 168
Continuous feedback, 104, 159, 163–164, 167–169, 171, 184, 211, 214–215
Cultural artefacts, 139, 149–151, 157
Cultural norms, 24, 140, 146, 150, 215

Cultural surveys, 139–140
Culture alignment, 23
Customer-centric culture, 49–51, 66
Dashboard, 162
Decision-making, 12–13, 19–21, 23–24, 27–28, 30, 34, 37, 40–41, 48, 54, 56, 61, 97, 102, 118, 122–124, 148–149, 176, 186, 201–202
Democratic leaders, 20–21
Design thinking, 190, 192–193, 195
Developing a culture change strategy, 171
Direct observation, 139, 146–147
Discovering the multitude of organisation cultures, 12
Diversity and inclusivity, 28, 37, 97
Diversity, equity, and inclusion (DEI) programmes, 175
Divisional organisational structure, 26
Employee engagement, 15, 21, 23–24, 30, 41, 55, 58, 66, 80, 101, 115, 139, 148, 165–166, 175, 177–179, 219
Employee engagement initiatives, 175, 179
Employee engagement and retention, 177
Employee feedback mechanisms, 139, 151–153, 157–158
Employee recognition programmes, 175, 179
Employee training and development, 175, 179
Employees, 35–36, 39–42, 69, 73–74, 76–77, 97–98, 108–109, 113, 115–117, 123–124, 127–128, 139, 142–147, 149, 151–152, 163–166, 175–178, 202–204, 215–217
Ethical and values-driven culture, 54, 66
Ethical culture, 13, 214
Exit interviews, 139, 177
External factors, 33, 35, 65, 98, 149, 151–152
Flat organisational structure, 48
Fostering open and honest communication, 210
Framework for designing culture change interventions, 172
Functional organisational structure, 26
Gathering collective input and feedback, 135
Groupthink, 123, 133, 145
Halo effect, 123, 133
Hierarchical culture, 12
How are high-performing cultures created, 56–58
How are shadow cultures created, 75–76

How to alter your organisation culture, 15–16
HR (human resources), 36
Identifying key players for collaboration, 127–128
Impact of high-performing culture, 58–65
Impact of shadow culture, 77
Inclusivity, 20–21, 28–29, 31–32, 36–37, 80, 84, 86, 97, 111, 113, 115, 117, 120, 164, 166–167, 169
Infographics, 162, 168
Innovation and creativity culture, 45–47, 66
Innovation-stifling culture, 72
Innovative culture, 12
Insights on organisation cultures, 149, 165
Interpreting the data collected, 159-160
Interventions, 109, 113, 116, 165, 172, 174, 178–179, 215–217
Interviews to gain insights and perspectives from employees, 135
Introduction: the six-step cultural change programme, 103–104
Is culture critical to your organisation's success?, 14
Leadership development programmes, 175, 179
Lean project management, 187–190, 195
Learning and development culture, 52–53, 66
Leveraging feedback for growth, 200–201
Listening to understand, 122, 124, 133, 210
Matrix organisational structure, 27
Measuring your organisation culture, 136–139
Methods for analysing culture data, 160–161
Mission, 7, 11, 17, 23–26, 37, 55, 58, 69, 73–74, 76, 97, 129, 136, 172, 179
Network organisational structure, 27–28
Onboarding and organisational socialisation, 178
Organisational identity, 24
Organisational structure and system, 174
Origins of culture, 13
Performance-driven culture, 43–45, 66
Performance improvement plans, 177
Performance management, 16, 44, 62, 177
Performance metrics, 61, 64, 139, 147–149, 157, 160

Physical environment of the workplace, 30, 37, 97
Political culture, 72
Presentation, 162–163
Project planning, 181–183, 213
Purpose, 15, 23–26, 33, 37, 54–55, 59, 80, 97, 103, 108, 114, 119, 126, 128–129, 163, 165 168, 173
Qualitative analysis, 160, 168
Quantitative analysis, 160, 168
Recognising and celebrating achievements, 203–205
Recruitment and onboarding, 177, 178
Regularity, 164, 167, 169
Results-driven culture, 13
Revisiting the collaborative commitment chapter, 163
Rituals, traditions, 32, 37, 97
Role modelling by leaders, 176
Role of shadow hunters, 107–108, 110
Scrum, 185–187, 195
Self-management organisational structure, 28
Shared vision for cultural change, 104, 127–128
Signs of a high-performing culture, 66
Signs of a shadow culture, 8, 73, 84, 98
Silo culture, 72
Social network analysis, 161, 168
Specialist culture models, 107
Start with the end in mind, 126, 205
Target audience, 25
Team-based organisational structure, 27
Team building, 33, 176
Top tips for embedding change, 201
Top tips for evaluating lessons learned, 198–200
Toxic culture, 72, 92
Transformational leaders, 21–22
Transparency, 13, 28, 54–56, 71, 80, 84–85, 90–93, 101–102, 108–110, 112, 115, 117, 164–166, 184–186, 188–189
Unconscious bias, 29, 76, 123, 133
Understanding organisation culture, 97–99
Understanding the cultural challenge, 111, 121
Understanding your organisation culture, 136
Using creative expression, 58
Value proposition, 25
Values, 7–8, 10–11, 15–16, 22–24, 31–33, 35, 45, 54–56, 73–74, 97–99, 101–103, 128–129, 135–142, 149–151, 153–156, 172, 175–177
Values and beliefs, 102, 136, 138, 176
Video, 88, 162

Wellness and work-life balance programmes, 176
What is a high performing culture, 39
What is a shadow culture, 70
What type of shadow cultures exist in today's companies, 71–73
Workaholic culture, 72
Written report, 161

Milton Keynes UK
Ingram Content Group UK Ltd.
UKHW020605211123
432934UK00012B/125